The Academic Librarian's
Human Resources Handbook

The Academic Librarian's Human Resources Handbook

Employer Rights and Responsibilities

David A. Baldwin

1996
Libraries Unlimited, Inc.
Englewood, Colorado

LIBRARIES UNLIMITED, INC.
P.O. Box 6633
Englewood, CO 80155-6633
1-800-237-6124

Production Editor: Heidi Olinger
Copy Editor: Janice L. Krygier
Typesetting and Interior Design: Michael Florman
Indexer: Linda Running Bentley

Library of Congress Cataloging-in-Publication Data

Baldwin, David A. (David Allen), 1946-
  The academic librarian's human resources handbook : employer
rights and responsibilities / David A. Baldwin.
    xii, 167 p. 17x25 cm.
    Includes bibliographical references and index.
    ISBN 1-56308-345-0
    1. Academic libraries--United States-- Personnel management--
Handbooks, manuals, etc. I. Title.
Z675.U5B278 1996
023'.9--dc20   96-19888
                                                        CIP

■■■■■■■ Contents

v

■■■■■■■ Introduction

How can you as an employer (dean, director, department head, manager, supervisor, lead worker) protect the library from problems resulting from violation of an employee's rights? The key is knowledge. No employer sets out to violate an employee's rights or, in effect, engage in an illegal act. Nor does any employer want to be sued or lose a lawsuit over an employment issue. At a minimum, what most employers want is to hire the best person for the job, have that individual come to work, perform that job in an effective manner, and, in exchange for an honest day's work, give an honest day's pay. Beyond that, employers also want to provide employees with a safe workplace and challenging, satisfying work.

The fact is that the U.S. government and the legislatures of the 50 states have been busily creating laws in the past 10 to 15 years designed to protect the rights of the nation's workers. The U.S. Department of Labor's Bureau of Labor Statistics reports that union membership is declining and that today only one in six workers belongs to a union. Five out of six employees are dependent on the government to protect them in the workplace, thus leading to an increase in employment laws in recent years.[1]

When jobs were more plentiful and less specialized, employees who felt they were not being well treated or paid well enough could often simply find another, better job. Today's library jobs have become highly specialized, however, and their number in many areas is few; for example, library employees who are expert at copy cataloging find it difficult to obtain other employment because this skill is not in high demand. The difficulties that may have caused a worker to change jobs in the past have to be addressed in the current situation because mobility is limited. Employment laws have been passed in recent years that allow employees to attempt to address such problems. It is important that employees know their rights and equally important that the employer knows them too.

What some supervisors have come to realize is that the laws have indeed changed in recent years, but for them it is unclear how those laws affect the employer-employee relationship. Those individuals may inadvertently violate an employee's rights or simply be immobilized for fear of violating someone's rights. Any library employee who supervises others and holds antiquated stereotypes about groups of protected individuals will quickly discover that if personnel actions are taken in violation of antidiscrimination laws, employees or job applicants may successfully sue. It is in everyone's best interest to know the law.

Administrators, managers, and supervisors must comply with many laws, executive orders, guidelines, and court decisions in the everyday management of the library. It is the constant concern of the library personnel/human resources office that all of the library's managers comply with current laws and regulations. The library's personnel/human resources office must be familiar with the actions of the Equal Employment Opportunity Commission (EEOC), the Occupational Safety and Health Administration (OSHA), and the Office of Federal Contract Compliance Programs (OFCCP) and must maintain close working relationships with the offices on campus that deal directly with these federal agencies. If the library's personnel/human resources office fails to keep staff apprised of current laws and regulations, the library may find itself burdened with costly lawsuits and large fines. The library can avoid these problems by constantly monitoring the legal environment for any changes in law, by complying with new laws and regulations, and by practicing effective management. Laws affecting employment are enacted by both state and federal governments. Often the laws are similar, but sometimes they conflict. Which laws applies to your employer and to the employee? The issue at hand may be covered by state law only, or by both state and federal law. When the issue in question is covered by one law only, that law applies. When state and federal laws are the same, there is no problem. When laws conflict, the law that affords the employee the most rights or protections is the law that applies.

Although many employment laws apply to all employers, other laws relating to employment apply only to those employers with a certain number of employees. For example, most federal civil rights laws apply to employers of 15 or more employees, while many state laws apply to employers with fewer employees. The primary reason that some federal employment laws apply only to larger employers is that Congress has attempted to lessen the impact of the laws on small businesses, and, in some cases, it would be difficult to statistically determine whether or not a company was in compliance.

Several terms used in this book need clarification. *Human resources* and *personnel* are used interchangeably, although *human resources* is the preferred term. The human resources office (or personnel office) houses those individuals involved in handling the centralized human resources activities in the library. Typically it includes the head of human resources, or director, who is usually a librarian. The human resources office staff are the individuals in the library who carry out the day-to-day functions of the office, which likely include overseeing the hiring and the paperwork for student employees, assisting hiring supervisors by handling the hiring process, and maintaining personnel files and records.

Librarian and *faculty* are used interchangeably even though not all librarians hold faculty status and, of course, not all faculty are librarians. Use of these words interchangeably is simply a reflection of the author's belief in faculty status for academic librarians. *Line managers* or *supervisors* are the people in charge of the employees who directly provide library services. The term *employee* refers to the person who is not the supervisor. The term *individual, person*, and *worker* refer to anyone in the organization. *He, she, him*, and *her* are avoided completely as are the terms *subordinate, paraprofessional, subprofessional*, and any term implying subordination.

Every profession needs a code of ethics. In addition to the *ALA Code of Professional Ethics*, human resources professionals in libraries subscribe to the American Society for Personnel Administration (ASPA) code of ethics shared with other professions.

> The practitioner must regard the obligation to implement public objectives and protect the public interests as more important than blind loyalty to an employer's preferences.
>
> In daily practice, the professional must thoroughly understand the problems assigned and must undertake whatever study and research are required to ensure continuing competence and the best of professional attention.
>
> The practitioner must maintain a high standard of personal honesty and integrity in every phase of daily practice.
>
> The professional must give thoughtful consideration to the personal interest, welfare, and dignity of all employees who are affected by the professional's prescriptions, recommendations, and actions.
>
> Professionals must make very sure that the organizations that represent them maintain a high regard and respect for the public interest and that they never overlook the importance of personal interests and dignity of employees.[2]

The goal of the chapters that follow is to inform the reader of how to avoid problems relating to the violation of employee rights. Chapter 1 is a discussion of the function of library human resources offices. Chapter 2 focuses on library management. The remaining chapters address the legal aspects of the employment relationship. In sum, the handbook is designed to provide the busy library manager basic information and background on employee rights and legal parameters of managing library personnel.

References

1. Patricia Brennan, *ARL Announces* . . . "Key Findings of the ARL Statistics 1993-94" (arl announce@cni.org listserv, April 11, 1995).

2. D. Yoder and H. Heneman, Jr., *PAIR Jobs. Qualifications, and Careers, ASPA Handbook of Personnel and Industrial Relations* (Washington, D.C.: Bureau of National Affairs, 1978), 18.

 # Chapter One

Library Human Resources Management

There are three ingredients in the good life:
learning, earning, and yearning.
Christopher Morley (1890-1957)

Libraries today are confronted with the challenges of meeting increasing patron needs, enhancing innovation, improving the quality of service, and raising productivity with budgets that don't keep pace. At the same time, libraries are being asked to provide an increased quality of work life and to comply with laws, guidelines, and court decisions that govern the use of human resources. Because people are the key to meeting these challenges, the personnel/human resources management function is an increasingly more important part of every manager's job. As a result, the personnel/human resources office and its staff become more critical.

Personnel or Human Resources?

In the past five to ten years, there have been tremendous changes in personnel departments in both the private and public sectors. Library personnel offices were not unlike offices in other organizations whose primary focus was on doing the paperwork needed for hiring and other personnel actions. The library's personnel staff served primarily a clerical function, making sure all of the right forms were completed and sent to the right office. Today, the library's human resources office is heavily involved in making certain that all personnel actions taken are in compliance with the law. In keeping with this change in emphasis, many organizations now have named their personnel function *human resources*. As personnel offices have evolved into human resources offices in other organizations, libraries have expanded their functions as well. Human resources is responsible for the following five functions:

1. Planning for human resource needs

2. Staffing the organization's personnel needs

3. Appraising and compensating employee behavior

4. Improving employees and the work environment

5. Establishing and maintaining effective working relationships

Although not all library human resources offices are performing all of these functions, the trend is clearly in that direction.

Planning for Human Resource Needs

The function of planning for human resource needs includes planning and forecasting the organization's short- and long-range human resource requirements and analyzing the library's positions to determine what is needed. The library's human resources office assists in identifying the number and types of employees required, their duties, and the skills, knowledge, and abilities that are needed. Human resources also helps determine how the necessary employees will be obtained, whether through internal promotions and transfers or through recruitment. The human resources office also helps determine training needs. The planning function is a relatively new function for human resources offices. Organizations are now more often relating human resource planning to goals and strategic planning.

Staffing the Organization's Personnel Needs

The library's human resources office continues to have responsibility for staffing once the personnel needs have been determined. Staffing activities include recruiting job applicants or working with the campus recruiting office, screening applications for hiring supervisors, and assisting supervisors by advising them on or helping to select the individual to be hired. The precise responsibilities of human resources offices differ, but basically the office is charged with ensuring that recruitment and hiring are handled efficiently and legally. The human resources staff is responsible for ensuring compliance with the university's hiring procedures and policies and with the laws and regulations relating to nondiscrimination in hiring.

Appraising and Compensating Employee Performance

After employees are on the job, it is necessary to determine how well they are performing and to reward them accordingly. It is the responsibility of the human resources office to ensure that the performance appraisal system in place is carried out by the library's managers. It is important that performance evaluations be conducted and appropriate actions taken when necessary. The human resources staff assists managers in taking whatever disciplinary action is necessary while ensuring compliance with the laws protecting employee rights. With the increase in employee rights and the high cost of replacing employees, libraries often try to assist employees in correcting poor performance, rather than attempt to terminate their employment. These actions contain potential pitfalls the human resources professional can help supervisors avoid.

Employees are generally compensated, at least in part, based on their performance as described in the performance appraisal. Although rewards usually are monetary, other kinds of rewards can be developed by an organization in the form of indirect benefits. The human resources office usually is involved in administering direct compensation based on performance evaluation and indirect compensation in an effort to reward high-performing employees.

Improving Employee Skill Level and the Work Environment

The human resources professionals in libraries have in recent years increased their involvement in three areas: (1) determining, designing, and implementing employee training and development programs; (2) improving the work environment, especially the quality of work life; and (3) working to ensure a safe work environment. Training and development activities are of all types. Included are programs designed to increase employees' skills and abilities and to offer learning opportunities to employees to help them advance in their careers. The primary purpose of improving the work environment is to benefit the employee and the library. Examples of improving the environment include working with quality circles, team management, and other plans for employee participation in decision making. It is also the library's responsibility to ensure a safe and healthful work environment. The federal regulations specified in the Occupational Safety and Health Act (OSHA) of 1970 are in place to ensure that the employees' work environment is safe and secure. The library's human resources office is often charged with the responsibility for compliance with OSHA.

Establishing and Maintaining Effective Working Relationships

This function of the library's human resources office involves four activities: (1) recognizing and respecting employee rights; (2) understanding the reasons and methods for employees to organize; (3) bargaining and settling grievances with employees; and (4) maintaining current awareness and professional development in human resources management. It is hoped that library administrators, managers, and supervisors will understand the laws governing the employment relationship and know what can legally be done in given situations. The book devotes little attention to the unionized workplace because there is already ample information available and because libraries generally have minimal union contact. A major function of the human resources professional is to resolve grievances and mediation issues. Lastly, it is important for the library's human resources professionals to maintain current awareness of the legal environment. Contacts must be made and nurtured with the various offices on campus that have responsibilities in employment and employee benefits. Human resources professionals also must develop and maintain contacts with other library human resources professionals through such organizations as the Association of College and Research Libraries Personnel and Staff Development Officers Discussion Group.

Roles of Human Resources

Library human resources offices can play several roles in an organization. The more roles human resources plays and the more it performs these roles well, the more effective it will be in improving the library's productivity, enhancing the quality of work life, and complying with the laws and regulations relating to human resources. Potential roles include policy formulator, provider and delegator, auditor, and innovator.

In order to effectively perform the four roles, the head of the human resources office should be in a position reporting to the person at the top of the organizational hierarchy and part of the library's decision-making group. This would allow the human resources professional to participate in personnel policy formulation and to have the authority necessary for fair and consistent policy implementation.

Policy Formulator

The human resources office can provide information to top management for use in planning. Useful to the library's planning and decision making are information on employee concerns, the library's work environment, training and staff development needs, and information relating to the university's human resources activities.

Provider and Delegator

The human resources office succeeds only if the line managers succeed. The human resources office assists administrators, managers, and supervisors in traditional personnel activities, including screening, interviewing, hiring, training, evaluating, counseling, promoting, and firing. These services are critical to the day-to-day operation of the library. The human resources office also advises management and staff on equal employment opportunity legislation and safety and health standards. To fulfill these responsibilities, the human resources office staff must be available to the managers, and the human resources professional must not lose touch with the library's managerial and operational staff.

Auditor

Because many of the personnel activities such as hiring, training, and evaluating are delegated to the library's managers, the human resources office maintains responsibility for seeing that such activities are implemented fairly and consistently. This is especially important in light of fair employment legislation and the increasingly sophisticated demands for accountability. The human resources office is responsible, therefore, for ensuring compliance and providing for a centralized office that has accurate information, the required expertise, and the support of the library administration in dealing with complaints.

Innovator

An expanding role of the human resources office is that of providing information to line managers and library administrators about current techniques and approaches to personnel issues. Many of the current techniques deal with improving the work environment and complying with the law.

Who Is Responsible for Human Resources Management?

In theory, everyone should be responsible for human resources management. The head of the human resources office is primarily responsible for human resources management, but the administrators, department heads, branch heads, line managers, and unit heads must work closely with the head of the human resources office and its staff in the day-to-day implementation of personnel functions. Cooperation between the human resources office and the managers is critical to effective human resources management. In addition, all of the human resources activities must have the support of top management in order to succeed.

Employees are increasingly taking a role in human resources management. For example, employees may be involved in peer evaluations and in developing their own performance standards and goals. It is not uncommon for employees to be involved in helping to develop their own job descriptions, and they are always involved in job classification studies. More and more employees participate in quality circles, total quality improvement teams, and in other teams that help them take an active role in management.

Today's Library Human Resources Manager

The library human resources administrator has all of the responsibilities of being a manager and providing support to the administration and the library faculty and staff in matters relating to human resources. These responsibilities involve all aspects of hiring and any action involving personnel up to and including termination, whether voluntary or involuntary. It is incumbent on the human resources administrator to fully understand the law as it relates to labor. The individual who chooses library human resources administration as a career will need to be able to work well with not only the library administration, but also all of the managers and supervisors in the library and the staff in the various university human resources offices, including the university counsel's office.

Bibliography

Association of Research Libraries. *Changing Role of the ARL Library Personnel Officer*. Washington, D.C.: ARL, 1978.

Beach, Dale S. *Personnel: The Management of People at Work*. New York: Macmillan, 1980.

Cargill, Jennifer, and Gisela Webb. *Managing Libraries in Transition*. Phoenix, Ariz.: Oryx, 1987.

"The Case of the Disappearing Typical Employee." *Profit Sharing* 42, no. 1 (January 1994): 4.

Coleman, Francis T. "The Personnel Challenge." *Association Management* 42, no. 7 (July 1990): 40.

Covington, Robert N., and Kurt H. Decker. *Individual Employee Rights in a Nutshell*. St. Paul, Minn.: West, 1995.

Cowley, John. *Personnel Management in Libraries*. Hamden, Conn.: Bingley, 1982.

Creth, Sheila, and Frederick F. Duda, eds. *Personnel Administration in Libraries*. New York: Neal-Schuman, 1989.

Cropanzano, Russell, ed. *Justice in the Workplace: Approaching Fairness in Human Resource Management*. Hillsdale, N.J.: L. Erlbaum Associates, 1993.

Davidson, Marilyn J., and Jill Earnshaw, eds. *Vulnerable Workers.* New York: John Wiley, 1991.

Dewey, Barbara I. "Personnel Costs and Patterns in Libraries." *Library Trends* 42, no. 3 (winter 1994): 537.

Edwards, Richard. *Rights at Work: Employment Relations in the Post Union Era.* Washington, D.C.: Brookings Institution, 1993.

Feliu, Alfred G. *Primer on Individual Employee Rights.* Washington, D.C.: Bureau of National Affairs, 1992.

Finkin, Matthew W., et al. *Legal Protection for the Individual Employee.* St. Paul, Minn.: West, 1989.

Fitzpatrick, Robert B. "An Employee's Checklist for Settling Employment Disputes." *The Practical Lawyer* 39, no. 7 (October 1993): 73.

Hames, David S. "Employers Beware: Workers Are Suing Based upon Nonstatutory Legal Theories." *Business Forum* 16, no. 3 (summer 1991): 5.

Hunt, James W. *The Law of the Workplace: Rights of Employers and Employees,.* 3rd ed. Washington, D.C.: Bureau of National Affairs, 1994.

Joel, Lewin G. *Every Employee's Guide to the Law: Everything You Need to Know About Your Rights in the Workplace—And What to Do If They Are Violated.* New York: Pantheon Books, 1993.

Koch, Edward I. "Employee 'Rights' Cause Concern for Managers." *American City & County* 100, no. 4 (April 1985): 87.

Lacey, Dan. *Your Rights in the Workplace.* Berkeley, Calif.: Nolo Press, 1991.

Levy, Andrew. *Rights at Work: A Guide for Employees.* Kenwyn: Juta, 1992.

Martin, Lowell A. *Library Personnel Administration.* Metuchen, N.J.: Scarecrow Press, 1994.

Martin, Murray S. *Issues in Personnel Management in Academic Libraries.* Greenwich, Conn.: JAI Press, 1981.

Maslow, Abraham. *Motivation and Personality.* New York: Harper & Row, 1970.

McGregor, Douglas. *The Human Side of Enterprise.* New York: McGraw-Hill, 1960.

O'Neil, Robert M. *The Rights of Public Employees: The Basic ACLU Guide to the Rights of Public Employees,* 2nd ed. Carbondale: Southern Illinois University Press, 1993.

Osigweh, Chimezie A.B., ed. *Communicating Employee Responsibilities and Rights: A Modern Management Mandate.* New York: Quorum Books, 1987.

Player, Mack A. *Federal Law of Employment Discrimination in a Nutshell,* 3rd ed. St. Paul, Minn.: West, 1992.

Rapoport, John D., and Brian L.P. Zevnik. *The Employee Strikes Back!* New York: Collier, 1990.

Rawles, Beverly A. *Human Resources Management in Small Libraries.* Hamden, Conn.: Shoe String Press, 1982.

Repa, Barbara Kate. *Your Rights in the Workplace.* Berkeley, Calif.: Nolo Press, 1994.

Ricking, Myrl, and Robert E. Booth. *Personnel Utilization in Libraries: A Systems Approach.* Chicago: American Library Association, 1974.

Rubin, Richard. "Ethical Issues in Library Personnel Management." *Journal of Library Administration* 14, no. 4 (1991): 1.

Sack, Steven Mitchell. *The Employee Rights Handbook: Answers to Legal Questions—From Interview to Pink Slip.* New York: Facts on File, 1991.

Sherman, Marc D. "The Continuing Trend Toward Employees' Rights." *CBA Record* 6, no. 5 (May 1992): 31.

Stebbins, Kathleen, and Foster E. Mohrhardt. *Personnel Administration in Libraries,* 2nd ed. Metuchen, N.J.: Scarecrow Press, 1983.

Sugarman, Jim. *Field Guide to Labor Rights.* Washington, D.C.: Essential Books, 1993.

Sullivan, Peggy, and William Ptacek. *Public Libraries: Smart Practices in Personnel.* Littleton, Colo.: Libraries Unlimited, 1982.

United States. President's Committee on Employment of People with Disabilities. *Employment Rights: Who Has Them and Who Enforces.* Washington, D.C., 1994.

Werhane, Patricia Hogue. *Persons, Rights, and Corporations.* Englewood Cliffs, N.J.: Prentice-Hall, 1985.

White, Herbert S. *Library Personnel Management.* White Plains, N.Y.: Knowledge Industry Publications, 1985.

Zigarelli, Michael A. *Can They Do That? A Guide to Your Rights on the Job.* New York: Lexington Books, 1994.

■■■■■■■ Chapter Two

Recruitment and Selection of Personnel

The employer generally gets
the employees he deserves.
Walter Gilby (1831-1914)

Prior to the enactment of equal opportunity legislation, it was not uncommon for librarians to be offered jobs by phone without having first had an interview, or for an administrator to simply say, "Hire person X," without advertising the position. Although today's complex employment process makes such scenarios seem appealing, most would agree that those weren't "the good old days." Employment legislation is designed to protect everyone, despite our complaint that there are so many rules governing current recruitment and hiring practices that must comply with the law. In today's legal climate, anyone who is involved in the recruiting, screening, and hiring of library personnel must be knowledgeable about the law.

Getting Started

Whether you are the library dean or director, department head, manager, supervisor, or lead worker, you may be the individual charged with recruiting and selecting a person to fill an existing vacancy or a new position in the library. The recruitment and selection of employees is guided by the procedures and policies of the library's governing body and by the institution's human resources department or unit. Such procedures and policies are designed to comply with federal and state laws governing hiring. Your objective is to find the right person from among those who meet or exceed the stated qualifications for the position, without regard to race, sex, age, or anything else unrelated to potential job performance. From the start you know that you may not advertise a job in any manner that would indicate a preference or limitation or otherwise discriminate against anyone because of that person's race, color, religion, age, sex, national origin or ancestry, or physical or mental disability. In addition, laws in some states prohibit employers from discriminating on the basis of marital status or sexual preference.

9

Is It Possible to Exclude Anyone?

Under certain circumstances, it is possible to exclude candidates when advertising a job opening. For example, if the job calls for it, a bona fide occupation qualification (BFOQ) can be stated in the job anouncement. A BFOQ or need exception is a narrowly applied exception in which a job requirement is specified that otherwise would be ruled discriminatory. A BFOQ must be reasonably necessary to the normal operation of the enterprise in order to be legal. An example would be to require a female for a position as live-in teacher at a girls' school dormitory. The exception applies only when religion, sex, or national origin is a bona fide occupational qualification. A case would be difficult to make for a requirement for race, for example, unless you were casting a movie that called for an actor to play the part of someone of a specific race. In *Dothard v. Rawlinson,*[1] the U.S. Supreme Court upheld a male-only requirement for guard positions in male maximum security prisons in Alabama. The Court referred to testimony that the use of women as guards posed a security problem in the all-male prisons.

Job Postings

Although advertisements may not include such phrases as "young person wanted," "persons aged 21-30," or "college student," they may include a minimum age requirement, as long as the age desired is under 40. For example, it would be legal to advertise for a person over the age of 21 if the ad is for a job serving alcohol, or, for a hazardous job, "must be 18." The Age Discrimination in Employment Act (ADEA) is designed to protect everyone over the age of 40. In fact, many state laws also protect workers under the age of 40. As a practical matter, unless the job requires a person over a certain age, any mention of age in the job advertisement is prohibited.

Institutional guidelines relating to the length of time and how a position must be advertised will direct your advertising. The rule is simply to make the availability of the job known to all, particularly underrepresented groups of people, and for a period long enough for individuals to reasonably apply.

Preemployment Inquiries

Whether applicants telephone, send in resumes, or simply walk in off the street, they must complete a job application form. Later, applicants may be screened for personal interviews. At the application stage or in an interview, applicants are asked a number of questions. Only certain types of questions are legal. Preemployment questions, whether written or spoken, must be directed at determining the applicant's qualifications for the position. Any questions not aimed at the evaluation of the applicant's education, training, and experience as they relate to the position are irrelevant and may be illegal.

As an employer you must be cautious in asking even the most routine questions of applicants, or you may inadvertently give a job applicant grounds for a discrimination or an invasion of privacy suit. Questions that are not allowable before hiring may be perfectly acceptable after a person has been hired. Asking a person's age, for example, is not allowed in the preemployment interview, but the same person may be required to give his or her age after being hired if that information is required for health insurance purposes.

Objectionable Questions

People are naturally curious and, when put in an interviewing situation, can forget that there are questions that shouldn't be asked. In a survey of more than 1,000 people, the National Consumers League of Washington, D.C., found that the objectionable questions most asked during the interview process were:

if the applicant lives with a member of the opposite sex;

the applicant's marital status;

the applicant's plans regarding having children;

the applicant's religious affiliation;

whether or not the applicant smokes off the job;

if the applicant has elderly parents; and

if the applicant has dangerous hobbies.

It is possible that the employers who asked these questions were either attempting to gather information that might affect group health insurance premiums or were ignorant of the fact that the questions were illegal. Regardless, these questions are objectionable because they are personal or discriminatory and have no relationship to the job.

Which Questions Are Permitted in the Interview?

The following are common questions you may or may not ask before and after hiring, with notes on their legality.

Questions relating to name before hiring:————————————

- You may ask the applicant's name and if the applicant has worked under another name.
- You cannot ask the applicant's maiden name or a spouse's maiden name.

Reason: Possible discrimination based on marital status or national origin.

Questions relating to address before hiring:————————————

- You may ask the applicant's current address.
- You cannot ask if the applicant owns or rents the current residence. Questions relating to how long the applicant has lived at the address and where the applicant lived previously and for how long are irrelevant and should not be asked.

Reason: Not relevant and could be used to unfairly single out minorities.

Questions relating to age before hiring:————————————

- You may ask the applicant if he or she is the minimum age required to perform the job.
- You cannot ask the applicant's age or any question whose answer would indicate how old the applicant is, either directly or indirectly.
- Inappropriate questions include:

    How old are you?
    What year were you born?
    What year did you graduate from high school or college?

Reason: Discrimination based on age.

Questions relating to age after hiring:————————————

- You may ask the applicant's age after hiring for employer-sponsored health insurance, or to ensure that the applicant is of legal age, for example, in order to serve alcohol or work in a hazardous job.

Questions relating to marital status or family before hiring:———

- You cannot ask the applicant questions that would indicate marital status or family orientation.
- Inappropriate questions include:

> Are you married?
> Do you have a family?
> What is your maiden name?
> What is your spouse's maiden name?
> Are you pregnant?
> Do you plan to have a family?
> What day care arrangements have you made?

Reason: Discrimination based on marital status, family, and pregnancy.

Questions relating to family after hiring:———

- You may ask the applicant for information about dependents who will be covered by employer-sponsored insurance.

Questions relating to citizenship before hiring:———

- You may ask the applicant if he or she is a citizen, as U.S. law allows preference for a citizen over an equally qualified noncitizen in hiring. You must be careful in this area, however, because it is unlawful to discriminate on the basis of national origin.
- You may ask if the applicant is authorized to work in the United States.
- You cannot ask if the applicant is a naturalized citizen.
- You cannot ask if the applicant is or was a citizen of a foreign country.
- You cannot ask if the applicant is planning to become a citizen.

Reason: Discrimination based on national origin.

Questions relating to citizenship after hiring:———

- You must ask the applicant to provide proof of eligibility to work in the United States.

Questions relating to national origin before hiring:———

- You may ask the applicant if he or she is a citizen, as U.S. law allows preference for a citizen over an equally qualified noncitizen in hiring. You must be careful in this area, however, because it is unlawful to discriminate on the basis of national origin.
- You may ask the applicant if he or she speaks a foreign language if it is a requirement of the job, a BFOQ.

- You may ask if the applicant is authorized to work in the United States.
- You cannot ask the applicant's nationality, ancestry, native language, or that of his or her family.
- You cannot ask where the applicant's parents were born.

Reason: Discrimination based on national origin.

Questions relating to national origin after hiring:————————
- You must ask the applicant to provide proof of eligibility to work in the United States.

Questions relating to group memberships before hiring:————————
- You may ask the applicant about membership in professional, trade, or other organizations that are directly job related.
- You cannot ask the applicant any questions relating to social or political group membership.

Reason: Possible discrimination based on national origin.

Questions relating to religion before hiring:————————
- You cannot ask the applicant any questions about religious affiliation or what religious holidays the applicant observes.

Reason: Discrimination based on religion.

Questions relating to religion after hiring:————————
- You may ask the applicant about his or her availability for work on religious holidays and if a religious accommodation will need to be made. You cannot refuse to hire if an accommodation needs to be made.

Questions relating to race before hiring:————————
- You cannot ask the applicant any questions about race or color.
- You cannot ask the applicant to submit a photograph.
- You cannot ask the applicant about hair, eye, or skin color on an application form.
- You cannot indicate an applicant's race on an application form or report.

Reason: Discrimination based on race.

Questions relating to race after hiring:————————————

- You may ask the applicant if he or she wishes to identify himself or herself as a minority for purposes of the employer's affirmative action program. Such identification is voluntary.
- You may ask the applicant to be photographed for a company ID where needed for legitimate purposes and if all other employees in the job classification are also required to wear a photo ID badge.

Questions relating to sex before hiring:————————————

- You cannot ask the applicant any questions about his or her sex or sexual preference.
- You cannot ask the applicant to submit a photograph.

Reason: Discrimination based on sex or sexual preference.

Questions relating to sex after hiring:————————————

- You may ask the female applicant if she wishes to identify herself as a female for purposes of the employer's affirmative action program. Such identification is voluntary.
- You may ask the applicant to be photographed for a company ID where needed for legitimate purposes and if all other employees in the job classification are also required to wear a photo ID badge.

Questions relating to disabilities before hiring:————————————

- You may ask the applicant about a disability as it relates to his or her ability to perform the job safely and competently.
- You may ask the applicant about a disability as it relates to the type of workplace accommodation necessary for him or her to perform the job. The applicant cannot be disqualified because you would have to accommodate a disability.
- You cannot ask the applicant if he or she has a disability.

Reason: Discrimination based on disability.

Questions relating to disabilities after hiring:————————————

- You may ask the applicant if he or she wishes to identify himself or herself as disabled for purposes of the employer's affirmative action program. Such identification is voluntary.

Questions relating to arrests and convictions before hiring:————

- You may ask the applicant if he or she has been convicted of a crime. Convictions can be the reason for not hiring because of their number, type, or relationship to the job, or because of how recently they occurred. Employers must keep in mind whether or not the applicant has been through a rehabilitation program.
- You cannot ask the applicant if he or she has ever been arrested or charged with a crime.

Reason: Not relevant and could be used to unfairly single out minorities.

Questions relating to military service before hiring:————

- You may ask the applicant about experience in military service as it relates to the job.
- You cannot ask the applicant about military service unless such experience is directly related to the applicant's ability to perform the job.
- You cannot ask the applicant about military reserve duty obligations.
- You cannot ask the applicant about military service for another country.
- You cannot ask the applicant about the type of discharge the applicant received on separation from military service.
- You cannot ask the applicant about his or her disciplinary record while in the military.

Reason: Not relevant and could be used to unfairly single out minorities.

Questions relating to military service after hiring:————

- You may ask the applicant if he or she wishes to identify himself or herself as a U.S. military veteran for purposes of the employer's affirmative action program. Such identification is voluntary.

Questions relating to height, weight, and other physical attributes before hiring:————

- You may require the applicant to take a physical agility test prior to hiring only if physical strength or ability is a BFOQ for performing the job and all others in the job classification are required to take the test.

- You cannot require the applicant to take a physical exam.
- You cannot ask the applicant for his or her height or weight unless such requirements are a BFOQ for the job.

Reason: Possible discrimination based on age, sex, race, national origin.

Questions relating to job experience before hiring:————————
- You may ask the applicant unlimited questions about job experience.
- You may ask the applicant the names and addresses of former employers.
- You may ask the applicant about former jobs held.
- You may ask the applicant about wages and hours at former jobs.
- You may ask the applicant about the dates of employment at former jobs.
- You may ask the applicant about gaps in employment history.
- You may ask the applicant about reasons for leaving former jobs.

Questions relating to education and training before hiring:————————
- You may ask the applicant about education and training, degrees earned, and professional licenses held as long as they relate to the position.
- You cannot ask the applicant about education and training that do not relate to the requirements of the job, particularly education and training in excess of reasonable requirements of the job.
- You cannot ask the applicant about dates of school attendance or graduation.

Reason: Possible discrimination based on age.

Questions relating to references before hiring:————————
- You may ask the applicant for job and/or character references.
- You cannot ask the applicant for references that would indicate religion, sex, race, age, or national origin, or otherwise provide information that could be the basis for discrimination.
- You cannot ask the applicant about dates of school attendance or graduation.
- You cannot check references without the applicant's permission.

Reason: Possible discrimination based on age, sex, race, national origin.

Questions relating to a lie detector test before hiring:————————
- You cannot ask or require the applicant to take a lie detector test. However, state and local police departments may request noncivilian personnel to take a lie detector test.

Questions relating to a drug test before hiring:————————
- You may ask the applicant to take an approved urinalysis drug test if the applicant is given advance written notice of your intent to conduct the test. Observation of the test is not permitted. Confidentiality of results must be scrupulously maintained. The applicant must be given a copy of a positive result.

As mentioned earlier, the library's human resources office will have developed an application form that is in compliance with employment law. The application form should include a statement to the effect that any misstatement is grounds for discharge at any time. It should also provide a place for the applicant to sign to verify the accuracy of the information therein. Courts have held that such misstatements are valid grounds for dismissal as long as the rule is not imposed so as to discriminate. It is an important safeguard for any institution's hiring process.

Background Investigations

In recent years, companies have sprung up that specialize in conducting background investigations on prospective employees for employers. These companies will check out such things as credit histories and criminal records. To date, it is not believed that any academic institutions employ such investigators. Although it is understandable that institutions would desire this service, because of the myriad of laws protecting the workers, they must be extremely cautious in using such services in the course of their hiring.

Consumer Protection Laws

Companies that do background checks on prospective employees must notify the applicant in writing within three days of asking a credit reporting agency to do a credit check. The Fair Credit Reporting Act specifies that notification be given that includes the fact that a credit investigation will be made and that the applicant has the right to request that the employer disclose the nature and scope of the investigation. The applicant must be given the information requested within five days of his or her request. The applicant must be told if a credit report was a factor in a decision not to hire, and the applicant has the right to know the name and address of the credit agency.

An employer can only use a credit report to verify employment. The Equal Employment Opportunity Commission (EEOC) has ruled that the use of credit reports adversely affects women and minority applicants and that the requirement for good credit might only be appropriate for positions that have responsibility for other people's funds, such as a financial consultant.

Part of the reason companies are cautious in their hiring practices is because they must protect themselves from a possible legal action resulting from "negligent hiring." Employers may be held liable for their employees' acts even where those acts have been found to have been committed outside the scope of their employment. An employer may be held responsible for the employee's act if there is some link between the job and the act, for example, if the job requires the employee to enter people's homes and while on the job, the employee commits a crime.

Personal References

Current or former employers who serve as a personal reference must be cognizant of the legal pitfalls entailed in the process. An employer may give a reference on a current or former employee at the request of the employee or a prospective employer. As an employer, you may give only factual, job-related information about the employee. You cannot comment on the employee's personal life or habits, whether or not the employee filed a discrimination suit or a workers compensation claim, or anything else that might be used to discriminate against the employee in a hiring decision. Some employers now respond to requests for references with the "name, rank, and serial number." That is, they will only confirm the most basic information about the employee: name, dates of employment, positions held, salary, and attendance. Other employers provide departing employees with a basic, noncommittal reference letter.

If you were to give a department employee you had fired a noncommittal reference and then subsequently give a negative reference to a prospective employer, you may be subject to a wrongful discharge suit. After all, if the employee wasn't bad, what was the real reason the individual was fired?

A number of factors limit what you can say in an employee reference situation. Privacy laws guard the confidentiality of personnel files, medical records, and arrest and conviction records. Defamation laws prohibit libel and slander, and civil rights laws prohibit employers from giving out information regarding an employee's age, sex, color, national origin, or disabilities.

Preemployment Tests

Some employers use preemployment tests to screen applicants for some positions. They include:

achievement tests to measure skills and knowledge required for the position;

physical agility tests to measure strength to perform tasks required for the position;

aptitude tests to measure general IQ;

personality tests intended to measure motivation, maturity, or interests; and

integrity tests designed to measure honesty.

The use of such tests must be nondiscriminatory. A test given to one applicant must be given to all applicants for the same position and under the same conditions. Tests cannot be used to discriminate, and tests that adversely affect the employment opportunities of any race, sex, or ethnic group are found to be illegal. The EEOC's "Uniform Guidelines on Employment Selection Procedures" provide a "four-fifths" or "80 percent" rule to determine whether or not a preemployment test has an adverse impact. The rule compares hiring rates for different groups. A selection rate for any group of less than 80 percent of the rate for the group with the highest selection rate will be regarded as reflecting an adverse impact on that group. Under the guidelines, employers may use the scores of tests in three ways:

1. To screen out those not likely to be able to perform the job successfully;

2. To group applicants according to the likelihood of their being able to perform the job successfully; and

3. To rank applicants, selecting those with highest scores for employment.

Although the use of employment tests may be very effective, their administration and justification can be very difficult. For those reasons many academic institutions do not use them.

Employment Verification (I-9 Forms)

The Immigration Reform and Control Act (IRCA) prohibits employers from recruiting, hiring, or continuing to employ illegal aliens. The Act is administered by the Immigration and Naturalization Service (INS) and requires that employees prove their identity and eligibility for employment in the United States. Before beginning work, the employee is required to complete an I-9 Employment Verification Form. The employer is required to review, sign, and retain the form in its records.

All employees, part-time and full-time, hired after November 6, 1986, are required to complete the form. Grandfathered in by the law are all employees who were hired before November 6, 1986, and have been continuously employed. Employers must verify the employment eligibility of everyone, not just those whom they suspect may be illegal aliens.

The 1991 amendments to the IRCA make it discriminatory for an employer to require any new employee to provide more or different documents than those required by the IRCA as stated on the I-9 Form, or to refuse to accept documents that appear to be reasonably genuine. An employer may be fined for knowingly accepting false documents and an employee may be fined for presenting false documents or documents belonging to someone else.

THE LAW IN BRIEF. Immigration Reform and Control Act (IRCA). ENACTED. 1986. SUMMARY. Makes it illegal to recruit, hire, or refer for hire any unauthorized alien; requires documentation of identity and eligibility of workers to work in the United States; and prohibits discrimination on the basis of national origin or citizenship status. Employer and employee complete applicable sections of the INS I-9 form. *COVERAGE.* Applies to all employers. *EXCEPTIONS.* Does not apply to employees hired prior to November 6, 1986. The antidiscrimination provisions of the IRCA do not apply to employers with fewer than four employees. *ENFORCEMENT.* Administered and enforced by the Immigration and Naturalization Service and the Department of Justice. *CLAIMS.* Must be filed with the Department of Justice or the EEOC. *LAWSUITS.* Private lawsuits may be filed within 90 days of receipt of a right-to-sue notice from the EEOC or within 60 days of notification from the EEOC that they will not sue on the employee's behalf. *REFERENCE.* Title 8, *U.S. Code*, sec. 1324.

The Hiring Process

The hiring process is critical to every library but it is fraught with potential problems. No one is immune to the adverse concequences that might result from sloppy hiring practices. The hiring decision, which is sometimes referred to as the million dollar decision, is not to be made lightly or carelessly. Like traversing a minefield, one has to move carefully, one step at a time, taking care that each step is legal. Awareness of the laws that protect the prospective employee is the first step in making certain the process goes smoothly.

Relevant Law

Other legislation referred to in this chapter is discussed elsewhere in this book:

- Title VII of the Civil Rights Act of 1964—Chapter 6
- Civil Rights Act of 1991—Chapter 6
- Title 42 of the *United States Code,* Section 1981—Chapter 6
- Americans with Disabilities Act of 1990—Chapter 6
- Age Discrimination in Employment Act—Chapter 6
- Equal Pay Act of 1963—Chapter 4
- First Amendment to the U.S. Constitution

Reference

1. *Dothard v. Rawlinson,* 433 U.S. 321 (1977).

Bibliography

Allen, Jeffrey G. *Complying with the ADA: A Small Business Guide to Hiring and Employing the Disabled.* New York: John Wiley, 1993.

Bequai, August. *Every Manager's Legal Guide to Hiring.* Homewood, Ill.: Dow Jones-Irwin, 1990.

Bielefield, Arlene, and Lawrence Cheeseman. *Library Employment Within the Law.* New York: Neal-Schuman, 1993.

Carper, Gayle Tronvig. "Negligent Hiring: Do You Know Your Employees?" *Journal of Security Administration* 13, no. 1/2 (December 1990): 73.

Cihon, Patrick J., and James O. Castagnera. *Labor and Employment Law.*, 2nd ed. Boston: PWS-Kent, 1993.

Cohen, Yinon, and Jeffrey Pfeffer. "Organizational Hiring Standards." *Administrative Science Quarterly* 31, no. 1 (March 1986): 1.

Coil, James H. III, and Charles M. Rice. "Managing Work-Force Diversity in the Nineties: The Impact of the Civil Rights Act of 1991." *Employee Relations Law Journal* 18, no. 4 (spring 1993): 547.

Connolly, Kathleen Groll, and Paul M. Connolly. *Competing for Employees: Proven Marketing Strategies for Hiring and Keeping Exceptional People.* Lexington, Mass.: Lexington Books, 1991.

Cook, Suzanne H. "Playing It Safe: How to Avoid Liability for Negligent Hiring." *Personnel* 65, no. 11 (November, 1988): 32.

Dunn, Patrick A. "Your Rights to References." *Security Management.* 35, no. 7 (July 1991): 67.

Cross, Harry et al. *Employer Hiring Practices: Differential Treatment of Hispanic and Anglo Job Seekers.* Washington, D.C.: Urban Institute Press, 1990.

Employer Incentives When Hiring People with Disabilities. Washington, D.C.: President's Committee on Employment of People with Disabilities, 1993.

Equal Employment Opportunity Is the Law. Washington, D.C.: U.S. Equal Employment Opportunity Commission, 1992.

Fenton, James W., Jr. "Woes of Negligent Hiring." *Personnel Journal* 69, no. 4 (April, 1990): 62.

Fragomen, Austin T., and Steven C. Bell. *1993 Immigration Employment Compliance Handbook: The Guide to Employment Authorization, Verification Procedures, INS Investigations, and Fine Proceedings Under IRCA.* Deerfield, Ill.: Clark Boardman Callaghan, 1992.

Friedman, Joel William, and George M. Strickler, Jr. *Cases and Materials on the Law of Employment Discrimination*, 3rd ed. Westbury, N.Y.: Foundation Press, 1993.

Green, Ronald Michael, and Richard J. Beibstein. *Employer's Guide to Workplace Torts: Negligent Hiring, Fraud, Defamation, and Other Emerging Areas of Employer Liability.* Washington, D.C.: BNA Books, 1992.

Greenwood, Mary. *Hiring, Supervising, and Firing Employees: An Employer's Guide to Discrimination Laws.* Wilmette, Ill.: Callaghan, 1987.

Half, Robert. *Finding, Hiring, and Keeping the Best Employees.* New York: John Wiley & Sons, 1993.

Herman, Susan J. *Hiring Right: A Practical Guide.* Thousand Oaks, Calif.: Sage, 1994.

Hiring Library Staff. Chicago: American Library Association, Office for Library Personnel Resources, 1987.

Jones, Randy F., Nancy A. Bereman, and Mark L. Lengnick-Hall. "The Effect of Job Impact, Job Interdependence, and Employee Characteristics on the Acceptability of a Drug Testing Policy." *Employee Responsibilities and Rights Journal* 7, no. 2 (June 1994): 103.

Kingsley, Marcie. "Honest Hiring: What Should We Tell Job Candidates About Personnel Problems?" *Journal of Library Administration* 17, no. 3 (1992): 55.

Lacey, Dan. *Your Rights in the Workplace.* Berkeley, Calif.: Nolo Press, 1991.

Modjeska, Abigail Cooley. *Employment Discrimination Law,* 3rd ed. Deerfield, Ill: Clark Boardman Callaghan, 1993.

Peterson, Richard B. "Organizational Governance and the Grievance Process: In Need of a New Model for Resolving Workplace Issues." *Employee Responsibilities and Rights Journal* 7, no. 1 (March 1994): 9.

Rogge, Melissa A. "Hiring Technical Employees." *Personnel Journal* 68, no. 11 (November 1989): 68.

Rubin, Richard. *Hiring Library Employees: A How-to-Do-It Manual.* New York: Neal-Schuman, 1993.

Sack, Steven Mitchell. *The Hiring and Firing Book: A Complete Legal Guide for Employers.* Merrick, N.Y.: Legal Strategies, 1993.

Singer, M. *Diversity-based Hiring: An Introduction from Legal, Ethical and Psychological Perspectives.* Brookfield, Vt: Avebury, 1993.

Stein, Ronald H., and Stephen Joel Trachtenberg. *The Art of Hiring in America's Colleges and Universities.* Buffalo, N.Y.: Prometheus Books, 1993.

Sullivan, Jim. "Finding, Hiring and Retaining Employees." *The Bottom Line* 6, no. 6 (December 1991): 16.

Tulacz, Gary, et al. *Lie Detector Use in the Workplace: Federal and State Restrictions.* Paramus, N.J.: Prentice-Hall Information Services, 1988.

■■■■■■■ Chapter Three

The Employment Relationship

My father taught me to work;
he did not teach me to love it.
Abraham Lincoln (1809-1865)

The recruitment and selection process has been completed and you have successfully hired a new employee for the library. That person has filled out the I-9 forms and reported on time for the first day of work. Now begins the employment relationship between you the employer and the new employee, a relationship that will invariably end in termination, either voluntary or involuntary.

It may seem strange, having just selected a new employee, to be thinking about termination. But it is an important part of the employer-employee relationship and an important consideration in establishing the employment arrangement. There are essentially two types of employment arrangements: contractual and at-will. In the case of contractual employees, the rights of both parties to terminate are quite clear. Those rights are spelled out in the contract and in the policies of the institution. In the case of the at-will employees, however, the extent to which employers are free to dismiss workers and the rights of those employees who are being dismissed have not been established in any final sense by the U.S. legal system.

Contractual Employees

In academic libraries, those individuals with faculty status or some type of professional status are typically contractual employees. The employer-employee relationship is defined by the contract and by the faculty/professional staff handbook. In many instances, the policies outlined in the contract or handbook have evolved to the point where they are almost identical at any academic institution with tenure and promotion regulations. In effect, an individual hired into a

25

tenure track position can plan to spend up to six years in a probationary status. Until a faculty member has applied for and been granted tenure, the institution may terminate his or her employment with sufficient notice, often without cause. On the positive side, once attained, tenure provides exceptional job security. The promotional system provides for advancement through the professorial ranks in recognition of research and publication accomplishments and, in some cases, seniority.

Employment At-Will

Typically, staff in libraries do not have contracts and therefore are what is known as at-will employees. What that means is that noncontractual employees are employed at the will of the employer and the employee. Either party is free to terminate the relationship for any reason at any time. The employee is free to leave for whatever reason and need not give notice. The employer, within certain restraints, may end the relationship through layoff or termination.

Traditionally, state and federal courts have supported an employment-at-will rule that specifies that an employer in a private institution may discharge an employee in the absence of a written agreement. This rule is based on the assumption that the employee may also terminate at any time without notice. Legislators have gotten into the act and passed laws making what was considered unfair practice by employers into illegal practice. The concept of "wrongful discharge" was developed to protect those employees who were being unfairly treated by employers. As a result, the employment-at-will rule is being modified through court decisions because courts have determined that there are specific situations in which at-will discharge is illegal.

Wrongful Discharge

The employer who unjustly discharges an employee may face a wrongful discharge suit. It has been estimated that win or lose, the average employer charged with wrongful discharge spends $80,000 to defend itself. An employer may be charged for wrongful discharge under any of the following conditions:

- The employee is fired in violation of the law.

- The employee is fired in violation of public policy.

- The employee's actions were safeguarded by "whistle-blower" protections.

- The employment relationship was covered by an implied contract.

• The employer had a tacit duty, because of the history of the employment relationship, to deal with the employee fairly and in good faith.

Fired in Violation of the Law

At-will implies that either the employee or the employer can end the relationship for any reason. That is essentially true for the employee, but not for the employer. Even though the staff member is an at-will employee, that person is protected by the provisions of employment law. For example, the Civil Rights Act of 1964, the National Labor Relations Act, the Fair Labor Standards Act (FLSA), the Occupational Safety and Health Act (OSHA), and the Americans with Disabilities Act (ADA) all protect the employee from illegal discharge. The Civil Rights Act of 1964 prohibits discrimination or discharge on the basis of race, sex, religion, disability, age, marital status, color, ancestry, or national origin. The National Labor Relations Act is designed to protect the employees' right to unionize and ensure that they will not be disciplined or discharged for attempting to organize. The aim of the FLSA is to not only guarantee employee rights to certain wage and hour considerations, but to protect employees from retaliation for asserting those rights. The OSHA is intended to guarantee a safe workplace and protect employees who file complaints with the Occupational Safety and Health Administration regarding safety concerns from disciplinary actions including discharge. The ADA, as well as many state and local laws, prohibit employment discrimination against people with disabilities, including those with AIDS and HIV infection.

Fired in Violation of Public Policy

An at-will employee may not be disciplined or discharged in violation of public policy. For example, it is in the public interest that employees serve on juries when called. In *Hodges v. S.C. Toof & Co.* (1990),[1] a former employee was awarded damages after being demoted and subsequently fired for a 13-week absence resulting from jury duty. It is also in the public interest that employees obey the law, so at-will employees may not be fired for refusing to break the law at the employer's direction. In *Sargent v. Central National Bank & Trust* (1991),[2] the termination of a bank auditor was found to be a wrongful discharge because he was fired for refusing an order to destroy or alter an audit report. The general rule was established in *Shaffer v. Frontrunner, Inc.* (1990),[3] when the Ohio Court of Appeals said, "There is an exception to the at-will employment doctrine . . . for wrongful discharge in violation of public policy."

Fired in Violation of Whistle-Blower Laws

At-will employees cannot be fired for reporting safety violations in the workplace or reporting their employers for breaking the law. These protections are guaranteed under whistle-blowing laws. For example, in *Haynes v. Zoological Society*,[4] an animal keeper was awarded damages when the zoo that employed her demoted her for reporting unsafe conditions relating to a bear attack. Other whistle-blower laws protect employees from discipline or discharge for filing workers compensation claims or for asserting other rights guaranteed by employment laws. The employer may find that any personnel action, however appropriate and necessary, will be examined carefully to be certain that action is not retaliation for the act of blowing the whistle.

Despite such protections, whistle-blowers run great risks. Although technically protected by the law, they may be branded by the employer as a troublemaker, ostracized by fellow employees, and find it difficult to obtain another job.

Proving Retaliation

How can library employees prove that termination was an act of retaliation by the employer? There are three basic steps involved in proving retaliation for wrongful discharge in court. The first step involves the presentation of evidence that retaliation has occurred. A prima facie case must be raised. For example, Employee A filed a workers compensation claim and shortly after was fired. The second step gives the employer the opportunity to explain why the personnel action was taken. The employer explains that Employee A was terminated for misconduct, a legitimate reason unrelated to the workers compensation claim. Employee A is then given the opportunity to present evidence that demonstrates that termination was in retaliation for filing a workers compensation claim, for example, evidence that two other employees who filed claims were fired, that all performance evaluations were positive, and that the employer used the pretext of misconduct for retaliation. The court then hears evidence from both parties relating to the action.

Implied Contract

The employment-at-will rule may be found invalid in situations governed by an implied contract. An implied contract is an inferred understanding of the conditions of continued employment. The employer's assurances, either written or oral, of continued employment could void the at-will arrangement and require the employer to show just cause in a discharge. Specific statements by a supervisor, such as "You will have a job here as long as you continue to do good work," have been found by courts to constitute an implied contract. *Kelly v. Georgia-Pacific Corp.*[5] provides a definition that is useful: "The court can consider the character of the employment, custom, the course of dealing between the parties, company policy, or any other fact which may illuminate . . . circumstances that may alter 'at-will' employment."

Fired in Violation of Good Faith

Employers are also cautioned that they may not terminate an at-will employee without cause after a long period of employment. Of course much depends on the nature of this long-term employment, but courts have found in favor of those employees because there has evolved an obligation on the part of the employer to deal with the employee fairly and in good faith. In one case, a California court awarded $1.7 million to an individual who was fired after 17 years with the company, saying that after such a long time, the employer had an obligation to treat the employee fairly.[6]

Employee Handbooks

Courts have found evidence of written commitments to continued employment in employee handbooks. Typically, the employee handbook is used to communicate rules and policies regarding safety regulations, overtime limits, pay periods, probationary periods, vacation leave, sick leave, and so on. Handbooks have been used by employers as a way to prove that an employee knew or should have known about a work rule that was violated. When courts began to find that employee handbooks included promises to employees regarding continued employment, companies responded by making four changes:

1. Including a general disclaimer in the handbook, such as "This handbook is not intended to be construed as a binding employment contract but only as a general source of information. The company reserves the right to make changes at any time."

2. Avoiding any statement that indicates a specific length of time for which the company intends to retain any person or group of employees in its employ, or gives any job security assurances to "at-will" employees.

3. Changing all references to "permanent" employees to "full-time" employees.

4. Having each employee acknowledge receipt of the handbook by signing for a copy of the handbook.

Probationary Status

The probationary period is that period of time anywhere between a month and six months during which the employer can assess a new employee's ability to perform the job. It is that period of time during which an employee can normally be dismissed without cause as long as that termination does not violate the law. In some instances, the new employee does not receive benefits during the probationary period. It is important for the employer to evaluate carefully a probationary employee for appointment to a regular status.

The Employment Relationship

Although *at-will* implies that the employee has a job at the will of the employer, and can be terminated for any reason or no reason at all, in practice the employer is limited in its right to fire without cause. Even though many employees are hired as at-will employees, they have the protections afforded by law. Employers often have good cause to fire people: incompetence, poor performance, insubordination, violation of company rules, excessive tardiness, excessive absences, or substance abuse on the job. The employer who has a justifiable reason and well-documented case for termination can fire an employee, even one who has passed the probationary period. However, an employer who fires an employee without having a strong, well-documented case will have difficulty in winning a wrongful discharge suit brought by the employee.

Relevant Law

Other legislation referred to in this chapter is discussed in the following chapters:

- Civil Rights Act of 1964—Chapter 6
- National Labor Relations Act—Chapter 4
- Fair Labor Standards Act—Chapter 4
- Occupational Safety and Health Act—Chapter 7
- Americans with Disabilities Act—Chapter 6

References

1. Tennessee Supreme Court, No. 233479TD, 1990.

2. Oklahoma Supreme Court, No. 70,796, 1991.

3. Ohio Court of Appeals, No. 48822, 1990.

4. Ohio Court of Common Pleas, No. A9005160, 1990.

5. 46 Ohio St. 3d 134, 1989.

6. *Lanoutte v. Ciba-Geigy Corp.*, California Court of Appeals, 5th Appellate District, No. F008571, 1990.

Bibliography

Coulton, Gary F., and Roger S. Wolters. "Employee and Management Rights and Responsibilities Under the Americans with Disabilities Act (ADA): An Overview." *Employee Responsibilities and Rights Journal* 6, no. 1 (March 1993): 55.

Dworkin, Terry Morehead, and Elletta Sangrey Callahan. "Internal Whistleblowing: Protecting the Interests of the Employee, the Organization and Society." *American Business Law Journal* 29, no. 2 (summer 1991): 267.

Egler, Theresa Donahue, and Erica Edwards. "Retaliating Against the Whistleblower." *Risk Management* 39, no. 8 (August 1992): 24.

"The Empowered Workforce: Needed: New Employee Bill of Rights and Responsibilities." *Industry Week* 243, no. 17 (September 1994): 37.

Estreicher, Samuel, and Michael C. Harper. *Cases and Materials on the Law Governing the Employment Relationship*, 2nd ed. St. Paul, Minn.: West, 1992.

Feliu, Alfred G. *Primer on Individual Employee Rights*. Washington, D.C.: Bureau of National Affairs, 1992.

Gilardi, Ronald L. "The Representational Rights of Academic Librarians: Their Status as Managerial Employees and/or Supervisors Under the National Labor Relations Act." *College & Research Libraries* 51, no. 1 (January 1990): 40.

Hames, David S. "Resolving the Conflict Between Clients' Privacy Rights and Employees' Equal Employment Opportunity Rights." *Employee Responsibilities and Rights Journal* 7, no. 2 (June 1994): 161.

Joel, Lewin G. *Every Employee's Guide to the Law: Everything You Need to Know About Your Rights in the Workplace—And What to Do If They Are Violated*. New York: Pantheon Books, 1993.

Koral, Alan M. *Employee Privacy Rights*. New York: Executive Enterprises Publications, 1988.

Merkel, Muriel. *Your Rights as an Employee: How Federal Labor Laws Protect Workers in Private Employment*. New York: Vanguard Press, 1985.

Moorman, Robert, Brian Niehoff, and Dennis Organ. "Treating Employees Fairly and Organizational Citizenship Behavior: Sorting the Effects of Job Satisfaction, Organizational Commitment, and Procedural Justice." *Employee Responsibilities and Rights Journal* 6, no. 3 (September 1993): 209.

Osigweh, Chimezie A.B., ed. *Communicating Employee Responsibilities and Rights: A Modern Management Mandate*. New York: Quorum Books, 1987.

Paul, Robert J., and James B. Townsend. "Wrongful Termination: Balancing Employer and Employee Rights—A Summary with Recommendations." *Employee Responsibilities and Rights Journal* 6, no. 1 (March 1993): 69.

Petersen, Donald J. "Trends in Arbitrating Falsification of Employment Application Forms." *The Arbitration Journal* 47, no. 3 (September 1992): 31.

Petersen, Donald J., and Douglas Massengill. "The Negligent Hiring Doctrine—A Growing Dilemma for Employers." *Employee Relations Law Journal* 15, no. 3 (winter 89): 419.

Piatt, Bill. *Language on the Job: Balancing Business Needs and Employee Rights*. Albuquerque: University of New Mexico Press, 1993.

Quinones, Ralph L. "The Need to Improve the Formation of the Modern Academic Employment Contract." *Employee Responsibilities and Rights Journal* 4, no. 2 (June 1991): 137.

Sack, Steven Mitchell. *The Employee Rights Handbook: Answers to Legal Questions—From Interview to Pink Slip*. New York: Facts on File, 1991.

Sepanik, Jani. *Drug Testing, Sexual Harassment, Smoking: Employee Rights Issues*. Washington, D.C.: Management Information Service, 1988.

Thomas, Steven L., and Vickie McGehee. "Faculty Bargaining in Private Colleges and Universities: Beyond Yeshiva." *Employee Responsibilities and Rights Journal* 7, no. 4 (December 1994): 297.

■■■■■■■ Chapter Four

Wage and Hour Laws

One generation plants the trees;
another sits in their shade.
Chinese Proverb

We tend to forget that there were times when an employee needed to receive his or her pay at the end of each day because there were no real guarantees that the laborer would be paid at all. During the Depression, the federal government stepped in to establish when employees were to be paid, where employees have to be paid, how much extra employees have to be paid for working especially long hours, how long employees can be made to work, and under what circumstances children could be employed. The Fair Labor Standards Act (FLSA) of 1938, which has been amended numerous times, controls minimum wages, overtime, equal pay, and the employment of minors.

Wages and Salaries

Wages and salaries are the payments received for performing work and are probably the single most important incentive for coming to work. Although individual library employees differ on how much importance they place on pay, clearly it is critical. Library managers need to understand how wages and salaries are determined and managed.

Although wages and salaries are often used as synonyms, they are slightly different in meaning. *Wages* refers to an hourly rate of pay and is the basis for pay used most often for production and maintenance employees or blue-collar workers. *Salary* refers to a weekly, monthly, or yearly rate of pay. Professional and managerial employees as well as faculty are usually salaried.

33

Hourly, or wage earning, employees normally get paid only for the hours they work, whereas salaried employees earn a set salary even though the number of hours they work may vary from pay period to pay period. Salaried employees are normally classed as exempt employees—exempt from the provisions of the FLSA.

Fair Labor Standards Act

The FLSA was enacted in 1938 and has been amended numerous times through the years. Before describing the provisions of the law, let's examine who the employees are who are exempt from its provisions. Exempt workers may include executive, administrative, and professional employees, as well as outside salespeople, and computer professionals. There are two tests—one long and one short—to determine whether you can be considered an executive, administrative, or professional employee and thus be exempt from the minimum wage and overtime laws. The long form is used primarily to determine whether or not lower paid (between $155 and $250 per week) employees qualify, while the short test is useful to determine whether or not higher paid (at least $250 per week) employees qualify.

The Long Test. ──────────────────────────────

You are an *executive* if you:

> spend at least 80 percent of your time managing a department or subdivision or directing the work of two or more subordinates;

> have the authority to hire and fire or to give recommendations regarding hiring, firing, and promotion of employees;

> routinely rely on your own discretion; and

> are paid at least $155 a week.

You are an *administrative employee* if you:

> spend at least 80 percent of your time doing office work; or

> are on the administration of an educational institution; or

> perform tasks requiring special training or experience with only general supervision or exercise general supervision over others; or

> regularly help your employer or an executive or another administrative employee; or

> routinely rely on your own discretion; and

> are paid at least $155 a week.

You are a *professional employee* if you:

spend at least 80 percent of your time doing work that requires an advanced degree or recognized artistic talent; or

are a certified teacher in an educational institution; or

do work that is primarily intellectual;

routinely rely on your own discretion; and

are paid at least $170 a week.

The Short Test.

You are an *executive, administrative,* or *professional employee* if you:

are paid at least $250 a week; and

spend at least 50 percent of your time performing the duties of an executive, administrative, and professional employee described in the long test above.

Computer Professionals.

To qualify as a computer professional who is exempt, you must be paid at least six and a half times the current minimum wage and your primary duty has to be one or more of the following:

applying systems analysis techniques and procedures, including consulting with users, to determine hardware and software functional specifications;

designing computer systems based on and related to user specifications;

creating or modifying computer programs based on and related to system design specifications; or

creating or modifying computer programs related to machine operating systems.

Independent Contractors.

One other major group of individuals who are exempt are independent contractors. Many universities use independent contractors for specialized work. The independent contractor is sufficiently free from the employer and normally is in a trade, business, or profession independent from that of the person employing him or her. The independent contractor is essentially a nonemployee who is paid for completing a specific task and is not paid any employee benefits.

Exempt Versus Nonexempt

Having examined how an exempt employee is defined for the purposes of classification under the FLSA, it is instructive to compare how the exempt and nonexempt differ from one another.

Nonexempt employees earn an hourly wage.

Exempt employees earn a salary.

Nonexempt employee hours are tracked by time clock or recorded on time sheets. Employees report hours worked and hours taken as sick or annual leave on the time sheet.

Exempt employees do not use time clocks or time sheets. Normally, exempt employees report the hours not worked, to be deducted from hours earned for sick days, annual leave, and so on.

Nonexempt employees are paid only for the hours reported as worked.

Exempt employees are paid a salary for the month.

Nonexempt employees are eligible for daily overtime, call-in pay, and guaranteed overtime.

Exempt employees are not eligible for such perquisites.

Nonexempt employees have a set maximum number of paid sick days, sometimes cumbersome work rules, and a formal discipline program for lateness and absences.

Exempt employees, except in government, do not have a limit on paid sick days and have few work rules and no formal discipline program.

Generally, exempt employees have certain benefits or privileges that nonexempt employees do not, such as fewer work rules, but exempt employees are not eligible for overtime.

Minimum Wage

Under recent amendments to the FLSA, employees must be paid a minimum wage of $4.25 per hour (effective March 31, 1991). Some states have set minimum wages higher than the federal rate. Employers must pay the higher of the two rates to its minimum wage employees. This wage is important to libraries in that student employees are directly affected by changes in the minimum wage. As of this writing, there are further discussions at the federal level about raising the minimum wage rate.

Overtime

The FLSA requires employers to pay time and a half (one and one-half times the regular rate of pay) for every hour employees work over 40 in one week or, in some states, for more than eight hours worked in a day. All exempt employees are exempt from the overtime pay requirement. In addition, other groups such as agricultural workers, car salespeople, taxi drivers, people who work on a commission basis, merchant mariners, drivers who work for employers who are subject to the authority of the Interstate Commerce Commission, anyone whose employer is subject to the Railway Labor Act, and radio and television personnel are specifically exempted from the overtime pay requirement of the FLSA. Hospitals and other health care providers are allowed to use a 14-day work period to calculate overtime, paying overtime for hours in excess of 80. Firefighters and police can be put on a "tour of duty," which means that they don't receive overtime pay until they work more than 212 hours.

State and local government agencies may be allowed to give compensatory time off instead of paying overtime. Unless the nonexempt employee is a public employee, he or she cannot agree to accept compensatory time in lieu of overtime pay. The FLSA requires that employers pay nonexempt employees overtime.

Jury Duty, Witness Duty, and Voting Time

Under the federal Jury System Improvement Act of 1978, an employer cannot discharge an employee for serving on a federal jury. State laws also prohibit employers from disciplining an employee in any way for responding to a summons to serve on a jury in state court. Normally, state employees have the option of either taking their regular pay or the pay offered to jurors, but not both. Federal law prohibits employers from making any deductions from an exempt employee's salary for being absent for less than a week, which would include time spent on a jury. The same rule applies when an employee is summoned as a witness for a trial. No federal law requires the employer to give employees time off to vote, but some states do make employers give time off if there is not enough time outside of regular working hours to get to the polls.

Child Labor Laws

When the FLSA was passed into law in 1938, child labor was a serious social problem in the United States. Although it is less of a problem today, the protection for children still exists. Under federal law, minors under the age of 18 may not work in any job that is considered hazardous by the Secretary of Labor. Included specifically in this catagory are jobs such as coal mining, logging, slaughtering and meat packing, wrecking and demolition, and roofing and excavation. Also included are working in explosives plants and any job involving radioactive substances.

Minors under age 16 may not work in mining, manufacturing and processing, in any job requiring the operation of motor vehicles, in public messenger service, delivery, or hazardous occupations. Exceptions include newspaper delivery, agricultural, and acting and performing jobs. Minors under age 12 cannot be employed except on a family farm.

Federal law does not restrict the number of hours children between ages 16 and 18 may work, but it does state that minors between the ages of 14 and 16 may not work during school hours, may not work more than 8 hours a day and 40 hours a week when school is not in session, may not work more than 3 hours a day and 18 hours a week when school is in session, and may not work anytime between the hours of 7 p.m. and 7 a.m.

Payment of Wages

It is not illegal to pay employees less than they believe they are worth. It is, however, illegal to underpay employees in violation of the FLSA or state wage and hour laws. For example, it is illegal to pay an employee for 30 hours of work when the individual has worked 40 hours. One potential area of abuse is in the misclassification of hourly employees as exempt so as to avoid paying overtime. On the positive side, classifying employees as exempt often gives them additional benefits, such as more annual leave.

Equal Pay Act

An important federal law that specifically addresses equality of the sexes in the workplace is the Equal Pay Act of 1963, which mandates equal pay for equal work. Equal work is that work that requires essentially the same skill, effort, and responsibility, done under similar circumstances. Fringe benefits are also considered as pay under the act, and therefore equal benefits must be provided to both men and women even if the cost of providing those benefits to both is not the same. Employers cannot lower the pay of one sex in order to remedy an unequal situation. The pay of the lower group must be raised. The Equal Pay Act does not require the employer to equalize pay in cases where different wages are paid according to a merit or seniority system, a system based on quality or quantity of production, or any other system not based on sex.

"Comparable worth" is a concept related to the Equal Pay Act. The act requires that people performing essentially the same job receive the same pay regardless of sex, while comparable worth states that people performing different jobs having essentially the same value to the employer should be paid the same regardless of sex. The justification is that historically female-dominated job classifications with lower wages should be compared with jobs characterized by the same levels of responsibility or requiring the same skill level or effort under similar working conditions.

THE LAW IN BRIEF. Fair Labor Standards Act (FLSA). ENACTED. 1938; amended numerous times, notably 1966 and 1972. *SUMMARY.* This act, as amended since 1938, regulates minimum wage, overtime pay, equal pay, child labor, and record-keeping requirements. The terms *exempt* and *nonexempt* originate with the FLSA—certain groups of employees are "exempt" from provisions of the law. *COVERAGE.* The provisions of the law, originally limited to employees of industrial and commercial concerns engaged in interstate commerce, were extended by the 1966 amendments to schools and hospitals, and by the 1974 amendments to agencies of federal, state, and local governments. Virtually all employers are covered by the act as a result of amendments. *EXCEPTIONS.* FLSA provisions on wage and overtime do not apply to executive, administrative, and professional employees. *ENFORCEMENT.* Administered and enforced by the U.S. Department of Labor, Wage and Hour Division. *CLAIMS.* Claims for unpaid wages must be filed with the Department of Labor within two years of the violation. *LAWSUITS.* A private lawsuit may be filed if a claim is not made with the Department of Labor. Employers can be fined up to $10,000 for violations of the child labor provisions of the FLSA. *STATE LAW.* Some states have laws prohibiting discrimination against workers under age 40 and over age 70. *REFERENCE.* Title 29, *U.S. Code*, sec. 201 et seq.

THE LAW IN BRIEF. Labor-Management Relations Act (LMRA). *ENACTED*. 1947. *SUMMARY*. An amendment to the Wagner Act, this landmark legislation, together with the National Labor Relations Act (Wagner Act) and the Labor-Management Reporting and Disclosure Act of 1959 (Landrum-Griffin Act), is commonly known as the Taft-Hartley Act. This act gives employees the right to organize and bargain collectively and prohibits employers from engaging in unfair labor practices. It established the concept of neutral arbiter. *COVERAGE*. Applies to all employers. *EXCEPTIONS*. Does not apply to agricultural workers, housekeepers, employees of airlines and railroads, independent contractors, and supervisors and other managerial employees. *ENFORCEMENT*. Administered and enforced by the National Labor Relations Board. *CLAIMS*. Unfair labor practice claims must be filed with the National Labor Relations Board within six months of violation. *REFERENCE*. Title 29, U.S. Code, sec. 141 et seq.

THE LAW IN BRIEF. National Labor Relations Act of 1935. *ENACTED*. 1935. *SUMMARY*. Commonly known as the Wagner Act, this legislation was intended to control and lessen the disruption to interstate commerce caused by strikes. It provides employees with the right to self-organize, to bargain collectively through representatives of their choosing, to engage in concerted activities for the purpose of collective bargaining or other mutual aid or protection, and to restrain employers from interfering with any and all of these activities. Amended by the Labor-Management Relations (Taft-Hartley) Act (1947) and the Labor-Management Reporting and Disclosure (Landrum-Griffin) Act (1959). *COVERAGE*. Applies to all employers. *EXCEPTIONS*. Does not apply in cases where age is a bona fide occupation qualification (BFOQ) of the job. *ENFORCEMENT*. Administered and enforced by the Equal Employment Opportunity Commission (EEOC). *CLAIMS*. Must be filed with the EEOC within 180 days of the violation. *LAWSUITS*. Private lawsuits may be filed within 90 days of receipt of a right-to-sue notice from the EEOC or within 60 days of notification from EEOC that it will not sue on the employee's behalf. *STATE LAW*. Some states have laws prohibiting discrimination against workers under age 40 and over age 70. *REFERENCE*. Title 29, *U.S. Code*, sec. 621.

THE LAW IN BRIEF. Equal Pay Act. *ENACTED*. 1963. *SUMMARY*. An amendment to the Fair Labor Standards Act, it prohibits discrimination in the establishment of pay rates on the basis of sex. It requires equal pay for equal work for men and women. Equal work is defined as work that requires equal skill, effort, and responsibility under similar working conditions. *COVERAGE*. Applies to employers of two or more workers. *EXCEPTIONS*. Does not apply in cases where different wages are paid according to a merit or seniority system, a system based on quality or quantity of production, or any other system not based on sex. *ENFORCEMENT.* Administered and enforced by the EEOC. *CLAIMS.* Must be filed with the EEOC, which must bring a lawsuit within two years of violation. *LAW-SUITS.* A private lawsuit may be filed if a claim is not made with the EEOC. *REFERENCE.* Title 29, *U.S. Code*, sec. 206(d).

Bibliography

Barnett, Edith. "FLSA Amendments Change More Than Minimum Wage." *Trial* 26, no. 9 (September 1990): 38.

Belrose, Bruce R. "Defining Fair Compensation." *Association Management* 42, no. 10 (October 1990): 63.

DeChiara, Peter D. "Rethinking the Managerial-Professional Exemption of the Fair Labor Standards Act." *The American University Law Review* 43, no. 1 (Fall 1993): 130.

Elwood, William E., and Cynthia A. Moore. *Employee Fringe Benefits.* Washington, D.C.: Tax Management Inc., 1993-.

The Fair Labor Standards Act of 1938, as amended. Rev. Aug. 1990. Washington, D.C.: U.S. Department of Labor, Employment Standards Administration, Wage and Hour Division, 1987.

Hart, Vivien. "MinimumWage Policy and Constitutional Inequality: The Paradox of the Fair Labor Standards Act of 1938." *Journal of Policy History* 1, no. 3 (1989): 319.

Lacey, Peter. *New Strategies for Employee Benefits.* New York: The Conference Board, 1993.

McCormick, Shawn C. "Minimum Wage and Overtime Pay." *Kentucky Bench & Bar* 56, no. 4 (fall 1992): 32.

Olson, Stephen. "FLSA Compensation Provisions: Avoiding the Pitfalls." *The Bottom Line* 8, no. 1 (February 1993): 10.

Perman, Lauri. *The Other Side of the Coin: The Nonmonetary Characteristics of Jobs.* New York: Garland, 1991.

Pols, Cynthia M. "The Fair Labor Standards Act: New Implications for Public Employers." *The Municipal Year Book* 53 (1986): 80.

Schiller, Bradley R. "Below-Minimum-Wage Workers: Implications for Minimum-Wage Models." *The Quarterly Review of Economics and Finance* 34, no. 2 (summer 1994): 131.

Silvergeld, Arthur F., and Mark B. Tuvim. "Key Court Cases/Recent Cases Narrowly Construe Exemption from Overtime Provisions of Fair Labor Standards Act." *Employment Relations Today* 21, no. 2 (summer 1994): 241.

Smith, Matthew M., and Steven H. Winterbauer. "Overtime Compensation Under the FLSA: Pay Them Now or Pay Them Later." *Employee Relations Law Journal* 19, no. 1 (summer 1993): 23.

Smith, Matthew M. "Overtime Pay Liability: The Unexpected Peril of Disciplinary Suspension Policies." *Employee Relations Law Journal* 20, no. 4 (spring 1995): 503.

Tremper, Charles, and Pam Rypkema. "Who Punches the Clock? Wage and Hour Laws Determine If Person Is Volunteer or Employee." *Business Law Today* 4, no. 2 (November 1994): 38.

United States. General Accounting Office. *The Fair Labor Standards Act: Extending the Act to State and Local Government Employees: Report to the Chairman, Committee on Labor and Human Resources, U.S. Senate.* Washington, D.C.: GAO, 1988.

Wolf, Charles B., and Richard A. Saldinger. "Avoiding Fair Labor Standards Act Pitfalls." *Profit Sharing* 41, no. 3 (March 1993): 14.

■■■■■■■ Chapter Five

Employee Benefits

*The ugliest of trades have their moments
of pleasure. Now, if I were a gravedigger, or
even a hangman, there are some people I
could work for with a great deal of enjoyment.*
Douglas Jerrold (1803-1857)

When considering whether or not to accept a position, one should always review the benefits offered by the prospective employer. Once given little consideration, employment benefits have taken center stage in light of escalating costs and national discussion of health care. Benefits are compensation offered or given to employees in addition to wages. They may take the form of vacation pay, sick leave, health insurance, or retirement plans. The fringe benefits of a position are an indirect perquisite that must be considered part of an employee's total compensation in exchange for work. Paid parking, reduced cost or free membership in a health club, and free checking accounts are examples of fringe benefits. For the purposes of this discussion, only the term *benefits* will be used.

Benefits

The employment relationship is a two-way street. Employers work hard to hire the best employees possible. To attract them, the employer offers what is known as benefits. These benefits have become commonplace over the years even though, for the most part, there is no law requiring that these benefits be provided. One exception relates to laws requiring employers to provide unpaid leaves of absence for certain family or medical crises. Benefits include group health insurance, paid vacation days, paid sick leave, paid holidays, retirement plans, and leaves of absence.

With the exception of family leave laws, benefits are established voluntarily by the employer. Once established, the employer is obligated to provide them to all employees in each job classification without regard to race, color, religion, age, sex, national origin, or disability.

Institutions attempt to accomplish a number of objectives with their benefit packages. Among those objectives are the following:

- Attract good employees

- Raise employee morale

- Reduce turnover

- Increase job satisfaction

- Motivate employees

- Enhance the organization's image among employees

- Make better use of compensation dollars

- Maintain a favorable competitive position

- Enhance employee security

Factors that influence the institution's ability to provide an effective benefits program include the size of the organization, profitability, union status, employee relations philosophy, workforce demographics, and projected growth/decline. Institutions strive to offer benefits comparable to those provided by competitors. Every institution must undertake a conscious ongoing assessment of the existing benefits program with an eye toward improving the program as much as possible.

Group Health Insurance

We have become so accustomed to employers providing group health insurance to employees that it is understandable that many assume it is required by law. The current national discussion relating to health insurance that, it is hoped, will be resolved by the time you read this, reminds us that more than 35 million Americans don't have health insurance. Although some of that group are unemployed, many are employed by small businesses who cannot afford to provide the benefit.

If the employer does provide health insurance, there are certain rules that must be followed. Generally, benefit plans require contributions from covered employees in the form of deductibles and/or copayments. Many state laws require employers who provide the benefit to provide certain mandated coverages, such as medical and surgical benefits, alcohol and drug abuse treatment, and mental illness treatment programs.

Employers are required, as of May 1, 1986, to offer workers over the age of 65 the same health insurance benefits offered to younger employees, and if coverage is mandatory, the employer cannot make the older worker pay more for the same coverage. In addition, if participation in the plan is voluntary, premiums charged to older workers cannot be higher than the actuarial tables show costs to be for older workers in relation to younger employees.

The Americans with Disabilities Act (ADA) ban on discrimination against workers with AIDS and HIV infection extends to health care and other employee benefits. As a group, women also receive some protections in the area of health insurance. The Pregnancy Discrimination Act requires that "women affected by pregnancy and related conditions must be treated the same as other applicants and employees on the basis of their ability or inability to work."[1] Employers must provide the same health insurance coverage to women who can't work because of childbirth or conditions related to pregnancy as they provide to all employees with disabilities.

Continuation of Coverage (COBRA)

The Consolidated Omnibus Budget Reconciliation Act of 1986 (COBRA) requires employers to offer employees the opportunity to continue their health insurance if they are terminated for any reason except gross misconduct. This law protects persons who have been dropped from the insured group for any reason, including voluntary resignation, layoff, or a reduction in hours that makes an employee ineligible to continue in the group. COBRA protects the spouses of employees in cases of divorce, separation, or if the employee is terminated or terminates employment. COBRA includes regulations relating to the employer's obligation to notify the employee of continuation rights, the length of time the employee has to accept or reject the offer, the maximum premium to be charged, the minimum period of extended coverage, and how the coverage may be terminated. In addition to continuation rights, the employee has the right to convert to an individual health insurance policy at the end of the extension of group coverage at individual policy rates.

COBRA covers all employers of 20 or more employees except churches and the federal government. Some states have additional laws to cover smaller employers. Employers must notify each employee and his or her spouse of their COBRA rights as soon as they join the group insurance plan. When an employee becomes ineligible for group insurance coverage, for any of the reasons given earlier, the employer has 30 days to notify the insurance carrier. The insurance company, in turn, has 14 days after receipt of notice to inform the employee of his or her right to continue coverage. The employee, employee spouse, or dependent has 60 days in which to elect to continue coverage. In the case of termination for any reason except death, the former employee, spouse, and dependents are eligible for 18 months of continued coverage by the group insurance plan. In the case of death of the employee or divorce or legal separation from the employee, the surviving or former spouse and dependents are eligible for 36 months of continued coverage. As noted earlier, termination for gross misconduct renders the employee ineligible for COBRA rights. Retirees or their surviving spouses who lose coverage within a year before or after the company sponsoring their health insurance plan goes bankrupt can continue coverage until their death and their dependents may continue coverage for 36 months thereafter. Employees called for active military duty may continue coverage during active duty. Military personnel called to duty who discontinue their health insurance coverage during active duty must be reinstated without a waiting period after return to work.

It should be made clear that those electing to continue coverage must pay the premiums themselves. Premiums may be up to 102 percent of the group premium. The right to continuation of coverage ends if the covered person doesn't pay the premiums; the employer terminates the group insurance plan for all employees; the covered person becomes eligible for Medicare; or if the covered person becomes eligible for another group health plan. Covered individuals may elect to convert to an individual policy at the end of the continuation period.

Sample COBRA Notice

The following letter is based on the U.S. Department of Labor's model notice, which must be given to employees to notify them of their COBRA rights. Although the form may vary slightly, the letter given to employees should convey the information contained in the model letter.[2]

Dear (Employee and Spouse):

Under the Consolidated Omnibus Budget Reconciliation Act (COBRA), enacted April 7, 1986, most employers who sponsor group health insurance plans are required to offer covered employees and their dependents the chance to extend their health coverage for a specified period of time at group rates under certain circumstances when insurance coverage would otherwise end. This notice is to inform you of your rights under the COBRA law.

As an employee of (Company Name), covered by (Group Insurance Plan), you are entitled to elect to continue your insurance coverage if you would otherwise lose coverage for any of the following reason:

* Your spouse loses his or her job or has his or her hours reduced;

* You are divorced or legally separated from your spouse;

* Your spouse applies for and becomes entitled to Medicare; or

* Your spouse dies.

The dependent child (or children) of an employee of (Company Name), covered by (Group Insurance Plan), is entitled to continue their insurance coverage if they would otherwise lose coverage for any of the following reasons:

* Your parent loses his or her job or has his or her hours reduced;

* Your parents are divorced or legally separated;

* Your parent applies for and becomes entitled to Medicare;

* Your parent dies; or

* You no longer qualify as a dependent under the plan.

Spouses of retirees also have the right to continuation of insurance upon the death of, or their divorce from, the retiree. In addition, retirees, retirees' spouses, and surviving spouses also have the right to continuation of insurance in the event (Company Name) files for bankruptcy.

To be eligible to elect COBRA continuation coverage, the covered employee or family member must notify (Group Health Plan Administrator) within 60 days of a divorce or legal separation, or when a child no longer qualifies as a dependent under the plan, or by the date coverage would be lost as a result of any of these events. (Company Name) must notify (Group Health Plan Administrator) of the covered employee's termination of employment, reduction in hours, or death.

When (Group Health Plan Administrator) is notified of the occurrence of one of the above "qualifying events," (Group Health Plan Administrator) will notify you that you have the right to elect continuation of coverage. You then have 60 days from the date you would otherwise lose coverage to inform (Group Health Plan Administrator) you want to continue coverage.

If you do not elect continuation coverage, your insurance coverage under (Group Health Insurance Plan) will terminate as scheduled.

If you elect coverage, (Company Name) must give you the same coverage provided to similarly situated employees or family members. You must be allowed to continue your insurance coverage for up to 18 months if your coverage would be lost due to termination of employment or a reduction in hours; or 36 months if your coverage would be lost for any other reason. Note: The 18-month period may be extended to 36 months if you are divorced or legally separated from a covered spouse, or the covered spouse becomes eligible for Medicare or dies within the 18-month period. The 18-month period may be extended to 29 months if you are disabled under Social Security disability rules and so notify (Group Health Plan Administrator) within 60 days.

You should be aware that, under COBRA, your continuation coverage can be ended before the full 18-, 29- or 36-month period, as the case may be, in the event of any of the following:

* You do not pay your insurance premiums within the required grace period;

* You become covered under another group insurance plan (except one that limits or does not cover a preexisting medical condition which you have);

* You become eligible for Medicare;

* It is determined that you are no longer disabled (and you had qualified for an 11-month extension of coverage based on your disability: insurance can be canceled at the beginning of the month following such determination); or

* (Company Name) ceases to provide group health insurance for any of its employees.

You do not have to demonstrate insurability in order to elect COBRA continuation coverage. However, you may have to pay part or all of the premium for such coverage. You must be allowed at least 45 days to pay your initial premium, which (Company Name) can charge retroactively. You must be given at least 30 days to pay subsequent premiums.

You also have the right to convert your (Group Insurance Plan) policy to an individual policy at the end of your COBRA continuation coverage period.

If you have any questions, please contact (Group Health Plan Administrator, Address, Phone). Also, please provide timely information to (Group Health Plan Administrator) regarding any changes of status (i.e., divorce, separation, etc.) that would affect your insurance coverage.

Sincerely,

(Library Administrator)

THE LAW IN BRIEF. Consolidated Omnibus Budget Reconciliation Act (COBRA). *ENACTED*. 1986. *SUMMARY*. Requires employers to offer to continue group health insurance coverage to employees and their covered dependents when their employment terminates for almost any reason except gross misconduct. Continuation is for 18 months. Employers must inform employees of their COBRA rights. The employee pays the entire premium. *COVERAGE*. Applies to employers of 20 or more workers. *ENFORCEMENT*. Administered and enforced by the Internal Revenue Service. *REFERENCE*. Title 29, *U.S. Code*, sec. 1161-1168.

Paid Days Off

Want to surprise and amaze your friends and colleagues? Tell them that their holiday pay, vacation pay, sick pay, personal days, and severance pay are not inalienable rights. In fact, their employer has established these benefits as incentives to attract them to their company. The employer is not obligated in any way to provide paid days off (except if they are offered to one employee in a job group, they must be offered to all employees in that group).

Paid days off normally include paid holidays, vacation days, sick days, and personal days. Contrary to what most people believe, employers are under no legal obligation to pay employees for any holidays. Of course, most employers do give employees holidays off with pay. In fact, employers give full-time employees an average of nine paid holidays per year. In addition, many employers give part-time employees holiday pay according to the number of hours they normally work each day, although there is no legal requirement that part-time employees be given any paid time off even if full-time employees are paid for holidays. Student employees in universities, for example, receive no paid holidays or any paid days off. Employers are free to set their own eligibility standards for paid holidays. They may require that an individual complete the probationary period before becoming eligible for paid holidays. There is also no requirement that employers pay overtime to employees who work on holidays unless those hours put the nonexempt employee over 40 hours for the workweek.

The employer has come to realize that employees often need time off to regenerate, to attend funerals, or to recover from brief illnesses. The employer extends the benefits of paid time off for vacations, personal leave, and sick leave not only out of generosity but to be competitive in the labor market. Although employers have great latitude in setting policies regarding paid time off, they may not discriminate against any individual or group in establishing those policies. Organizations vary on whether or not they allow employees to accrue paid time off and whether an employee may be paid for those days on termination of employment. If employers have a policy on paying for accrued days, it must be applied evenly. If not evenly applied, employees may sue for double the unpaid amount under federal and state wage and hour laws.

Maternity Leave

Federal law requires employers to provide leave for family emergencies. The Pregnancy Discrimination Act, an amendment to Title VII of the Civil Rights Act of 1964, prohibits discrimination against employees based on pregnancy. The law covers all employers of more than 15 employees and requires that "women affected by pregnancy, childbirth or related medical conditions . . . be treated the same for all employment-related purposes . . . as other personnel" who are not pregnant but are "similar in their ability or inability to work."[3] Under the terms of the law, the employer can't require a woman to take a maternity leave of a certain length that bears no relation to the woman's ability or inability to work. The employer must offer reinstatement to the same or an equivalent job with the same benefits and seniority to a woman returning from maternity leave. The employer must offer leaves of absence for pregnancy- and childbirth-related disabilities under the same terms as it offered them for other disabilities.

THE LAW IN BRIEF. Pregnancy Discrimination Act of 1978. *ENACTED.* 1978. *SUMMARY.* An amendment to Title VII of the Civil Rights Act of 1964, it prohibits employers from discriminating against employees based on pregnancy. It requires that "women affected by pregnancy, childbirth or related medical conditions . . . be treated the same for all employment-related purposes . . . as other personnel" who are not pregnant but are "similar in their ability or inability to work."[4] *COVERAGE.* Applies to all public employers and all private employers of 15 or more employees. *EXCEPTIONS.* To be eligible, employees must have been employed for at least a year and have worked at least 1,250 hours within the previous 12 months. *ENFORCEMENT.* Administered and enforced by the Equal Employment Opportunity Commission (EEOC). *CLAIMS.* Must be filed with the EEOC within 180 days of the violation. *LAWSUITS.* Private lawsuits may be filed within 90 days of receipt of a right-to-sue notice from the EEOC or within 60 days of notification from EEOC that it will not sue on the employee's behalf. *REFERENCE.* Title 42, *U.S. Code,* sec. 2000e.

Family and Medical Leave

The Family and Medical Leave law was enacted in 1993 to require that employers grant eligible employees time off without pay for serious illness, for the birth or adoption of a child, or to take care of an ill child, spouse, or parent. In order to be eligible for leave without pay, the employee must have been employed for at least a year or, if part-time, must have worked at least 1,250 hours during the past year. Employees are eligible for this benefit once per year. The act is administered and enforced by the U.S. Department of Labor.

THE LAW IN BRIEF. Family and Medical Leave Act of 1993. *ENACTED*. 1993. *SUMMARY*. Provides that eligible employees be given up to 12 weeks of unpaid leave for their own serious illness, the birth or adoption of a child, or the care of a seriously ill child, spouse, or parent. *COVERAGE*. Applies to all public employers and all private employers of 50 or more employees. *EXCEPTIONS*. To be eligible, employees must have been employed for at least a year and have worked at least 1,250 hours within the previous 12 months. *ENFORCEMENT*. Administered and enforced by the U.S. Department of Labor. *REFERENCE*. Public Law 1033.

Military Leave

Federal law also protects the employment rights of members of the national guard and military reserves. The Vietnam Era Veterans' Readjustment Assistance Act and the Veterans' Reemployment Act were established to provide those protections. Employers must allow employees leaves of absence during work hours to attend reserve or national guard meetings, training sessions, and drills. Employers are required to keep reservists' jobs open when they are called to active duty, and they are required to reinstate reservists when they complete their tour of duty. When called to active duty, reservists should request a leave of absence in writing and show their orders to the employer, although neither is required by law. Reservists are only required to verbally inform the employer of their call to duty. Employers do not have to pay reservists while they are on active duty. Employers do not have to continue group health insurance for the reservist on active duty, although employers do have to offer COBRA benefits. Reservists may continue coverage during active duty, although the military covers the reservist and dependents during the tour of duty. Reservists who discontinue their health insurance coverage must be reinstated without a waiting period after returning to work. For the purpose of vesting requirements of pension benefits, military service cannot be considered as an interruption of continuous employment. Finally, an employer cannot require an employee reservist to use earned annual leave while on active duty.

THE LAW IN BRIEF. Vietnam Era Veterans' Readjustment Assistance Act. ENACTED. 1974. SUMMARY. Requires federal contractors and subcontractors to take affirmative action to employ, and advance in employment, qualified disabled veterans and veterans of the Vietnam era. A Vietnam-era veteran is defined as a person who served on active duty for a period of more than 180 days, any part of which occurred between August 5, 1964, and May 7, 1975, and was discharged or released therefrom with other than a dishonorable discharge or was discharged or released from active duty for a service-connected disability during the same time period. Prohibits discipline or discharge of military reservists and members of the National Guard who must be absent for training and gives certain reemployment rights to employees who enlist in the military. COVERAGE. Applies to federal contractors and subcontractors. ENFORCEMENT. Administered and enforced by the Veterans Employment Service. CLAIMS. Must be filed with the local branch of the Veterans Employment Service. Disabled veterans may file discrimination claims with the EEOC. REFERENCE. Title 38, U.S. Code, sec. 2011 et seq.

Retirement Plans

As with most benefits, the employer's sponsorship of a retirement plan is left to the discretion of the employer, except in the case of public institutions and organizations. The advantages to the employer and the employee are great when the tax advantages to both are considered. Organizations offer retirement plans to attract and hold good employees, and employees benefit from having the contributions and the earnings of a retirement plan's investments deferred until those benefits are paid, likely at a time when the employee will be in a lower tax bracket.

The Employee Retirement Income Security Act (ERISA) covers all employers who offer a pension or retirement plan to employees. Its provisions govern who may participate, and the vesting of employer contributions. ERISA includes a number of employer reporting and disclosure requirements to the federal agencies charged with administering and enforcing the act: the U.S. Treasury Department, the Internal Revenue Service, and the Pension Benefit Guaranty Corporation.

Generally, there are two basic types of retirement plans: the more traditional defined benefit plan, which commits employers to pay a certain benefit amount when the employee retires, and the defined contribution plan, which commits the employer to contributing a certain amount each year. Defined benefit plans require the employer to pay out a set amount regardless of how well or badly the plan's investments perform. The defined contribution plans are tied to profits and lessen the risk to the plan's sponsor.

Examples of defined contribution plans include profit-sharing plans, stock-option plans, 401(k) plans, and Individual Retirement Accounts (IRAs). In profit-sharing plans, a designated percentage of company profits is added to employee contributions to a trust fund that finances benefits to retirees. In stock-option plans, employees are either given stock in the company or the option to purchase shares. Section 401(k) of the Internal Revenue Code allows employees to defer payment of taxes on part of their wages until retirement. The deferred amount, matched to some degree by some employers, is invested for retirement by the employee in mutual funds, for example. At least 70 percent of the institution's employees have to participate for the company's contributions to be tax deductible by the employer. Individual Retirement Accounts (IRAs) are normally thought of as personal retirement plans although employers may sponsor IRAs for employees. In all of these examples, the extent of the employee's retirement benefits depends on the investment vehicle's performance, whether it be the company's performance (stocks), the stock market's performance, or interest rates.

Once the employer has established a retirement or pension plan, the employees are entitled to participate if they are 21 years old and have worked for the employer for a year. However an employer may require employees to have been employed for two years if, when they join the plan, they become 100 percent vested immediately. A second exemption applies to tax-exempt educational institutions, which may require their employees to be 26 years of age to participate in the plan.

After the employee becomes an official participant in the retirement or pension plan, the first questions usually relate to what happens to the contributions if the employee leaves the company before retirement. The answers to those questions relate to vesting, which refers to the point at which the employee has a right to the contributions made to the plan. Although the employee may not be able to take the cash upon leaving, he or she retains a nonforfeitable right to those benefits upon retirement regardless of what company or institution employs him or her at the time. Most retirement plans involve contributions by both the employee and the employer. The employee is 100 percent vested in his or her own contributions immediately. That is, the employee owns those funds and any earnings made by those funds. The employee has a right to the employer's contributions when the employee becomes vested. The rules for vesting changed for plan years beginning in 1989. For those plans or those following, the employee becomes vested immediately if the employer requires service of more than one year for participation in the plan. If the employee is eligible to participate at age 21 or after working for the institution for a year, there are two vesting options: (1) The employee becomes 100 percent vested after five years with the institution; or (2) the employee becomes 20 percent vested after three years and 20 percent more vested after each additional year with the institution, becoming fully vested after seven years. For plan years that began in 1988 or before, the basic requirement was that employees be at least 50 percent vested after 10 years and 100 percent vested after 15 years.

If an employee leaves after being vested, it may not be possible for that person to receive a lump sum payment. Some plans require that an employee actually retire before claiming any benefit. If the employee leaves before becoming fully vested and returns, that employee will retain credit for previous employment years. The employee on maternity or paternity leave will continue to accrue credit toward vesting, up to 501 hours.

THE LAW IN BRIEF. Employee Retirement Income Security Act (ERISA). *ENACTED*. 1974. *SUMMARY*. The purposes of the act are to provide fair standards for participation and vesting; to provide safety of assets through funding, insurance, and fiduciary standards; to provide a guide for fiduciary conduct; and to provide adequate reporting and disclosure. The act provides mandatory rules on all pensions, profit-sharing, stock-bonus, and some welfare plans. ERISA covers the rights of employees to participate and be vested under pension plans and sets standards for the management of funds. *COVERAGE*. Applies to all employers who sponsor pension or retirement plans for their employees. All private employee benefit plans of companies involved in interstate commerce are covered by the act. *ENFORCEMENT*. Administered and enforced by the U.S. Department of Labor, the U.S. Treasury Department, the Internal Revenue Service, and the Pension Benefit Guaranty Corporation. *LAWSUITS*. Individuals may file private lawsuits if their ERISA rights are violated. *REFERENCE*. Title 29, *U.S. Code*, sec. 1001 et seq.

THE LAW IN BRIEF. Older Workers Benefit Protection Act (OWBPA) of 1990. *ENACTED*. 1990. *SUMMARY*. Prohibits age discrimination in employee benefits and establishes minimum standards for determining the validity of waivers of age claims. Provides "equal benefit or equal cost" standard—that older workers be given benefits that are at least equal to those provided to younger workers unless the employer can prove that the cost would be more for older workers than for younger workers. *COVERAGE*. Applies to employers of 20 or more workers. *EXCEPTIONS*. Early retirement incentive plans are exempted from the "equal benefit or equal cost" standard. *ENFORCEMENT*. Administered and enforced by the EEOC. *CLAIMS*. Must be filed with the EEOC within 180 days of the violation. *LAWSUITS*. Private lawsuits may be filed within 90 days of receipt of a right-to-sue notice from the EEOC or within 60 days of notification from the EEOC that it will not sue on the employee's behalf. *REFERENCE*. 29 *U.S. Code*, sec. 621.

References

1. *Americans with Disabilities Act of 1990* (PL 101-336, 26 July 1990), 104 *United States Statutes at Large:* 331.

2. *Consolidated Omnibus Budget Reconciliation Act of 1986* (PL 99-272, 7 April 1986), *United States Statutes at Large:* 227-228.

3. *Pregancy Discrimination Act* (PL 95-272, 31 Oct. 1978), 96 *United States Statutes at Large:* 2076.

4. Ibid.

Bibliography

Assistance and Benefits Information Directory: A Guide to Programs and Printed Materials Describing Assistance Programs, Benefits, and Services Offered to Individuals by Federal and State Agencies. Detroit, Mich.: Omnigraphics, 1992.

"Firms Must Guard Rights of Employee Reservists." *American Consulting Engineer* 2, no. 1 (winter 1991): 46.

Gottlich, Vicki. "ERISA Preemption: A Stumbling Block to State Health Care Reform." *Clearinghouse Review* 26, no. 11 (March 1993): 1469.

————. "Twenty Years of ERISA: So What?" *Clearinghouse Review* 28, no. 6 (October 1994): 678.

Humphreys, Richard W. "Defined Benefit Versus Defined Contribution Pension Plans: How Are the Interests of Employees and the Public Best Served?" *Employee Responsibilities and Rights Journal* 6, no. 1 (March 1993): 21.

Kaplan, Eileen, and Cherlyn S. Granrose. "Factors Influencing Women's Decisions to Leave an Organization Following Childbirth." *Employee Responsibilities and Rights Journal* 6, no. 1 (March 1993): 45.

Lavelle, John H. "Benefiting from Benefits." *American School & University* 63, no. 9 (May 1991): 54.

Maatman, Gerald L., Jr., and Andrew J. Boling. "What You Should Know About the Family and Medical Leave Act." *The Practical Lawyer* 39, no. 5 (July 1993): 21.

Marcus, Richard L. *Family and Medical Leave: Policies and Procedures.* New York: Wiley Law Publications, 1994.

National Committee for Employer Support of the Guard and Reserve. *Job Rights for Reservists and Members of the National Guard.* Arlington, Va.: The Committee, 1993.

Nobles, Richard. *Pensions, Employment, and the Law.* New York: Oxford University Press, 1993.

Ormsby, Joseph G., Geralyn McClure Franklin, and Robert K. Robinson. "AIDS in the Workplace: Implications for Human Resource Managers." *S.A.M. Advanced Management Journal* 55, no. 2 (spring 1990): 23.

Scharlach, Andrew E., Stephanie L. Sansom, and Janice Stanger. "The Family and Medical Leave Act of 1993: How Fully Is Business Complying?" *California Management Review* 37, no. 2 (winter 1995): 66.

Shultz, Paul T., and Karen L. Looram. "Employee Benefits—Managing Workers' Compensation Medical Costs: A State-by-State Guide." *Employee Relations Law Journal* 19, no. 3 (winter 1993): 251.

Sohlgren, Eric C. "Group Health Benefits Discrimination Against AIDS Victims: Falling Through the Gaps of Federal Law—ERISA, the Rehabilitation Act and the Americans with Disabilities Act." *Loyola of Los Angeles Law Review* 24, no. 4 (June 1991): 1247.

Sprotzer, Ira B. "Parental and Family Leave Laws: A Review and Analysis." *Employee Benefits Journal* 15, no. 4 (December 1990): 12.

Walworth, Carla R., and Margaret J. Strange. "Serving Two Masters: The Interaction Between Family and Medical Leave Acts and the ADA." *Employee Relations Law Journal* 18, no. 3 (winter 1992): 461.

■■■■■■■ Chapter Six

Discrimination Laws

By working faithfully eight hours a day,
you may eventually get to be a boss and
work twelve hours a day.
Robert Frost (1874-1963)

The most powerful antidiscrimination law governing the work-place is Title VII of the Civil Rights Act of 1964. It outlawed discrimination based on race, skin color, religious beliefs, or national origin. Title VII also created the Equal Employment Opportunity Commission (EEOC) to administer and enforce the antidiscrimination law. Since 1964, a number of additional laws have been enacted to provide additional protections for individuals. Included are laws prohibiting discrimination based on age, gender, pregnancy, and disability. Although it is important for all library personnel to have a basic understanding of the antidiscrimination laws, it is a requirement that library human resources managers know the law in order to assist supervisors, managers, and administrators not only in hiring, but in performance appraisal, discipline, and discharge situations.

Discrimination

Fully 70 percent of the workforce are members of at least one protected group; that does not include those who are protected from reverse discrimination (discrimination against someone who is not a member of any protected group). Among those protected by discrimination laws include females, members of racial minority groups, persons over age 40, and persons from other countries. Individuals are also protected under the law from discrimination based on religion or disability. Among the laws designed to protect individuals from employment discrimination are the Civil Rights Act of

57

1991; Title VII of the Civil Rights Act of 1964; Title 42 of the *United States Code,* Section 1981; the Americans with Disabilities Act (ADA) of 1990; the Age Discrimination in Employment Act (ADEA); the Equal Pay Act of 1963; and the First Amendment to the U.S. Constitution.

Civil Rights

Simply stated, Title VII of the Civil Rights Act of 1964 prohibits an employer from refusing to hire or from discriminating against an employee on the job because of the employee's race, color, religion, sex, or national origin. Although the law applies only to employers with 15 or more employees, many state laws have extended those prohibitions to smaller employers.

The 1964 Civil Rights Act, with all of its amendments added during the next 25 years, serves to protect employees from discriminatory acts by employers. The 1964 Civil Rights Act was limited somewhat when in 1989 the U.S. Supreme Court ruled in *Patterson v. McLean Credit Union*[1] that the statute barred discrimination only in the formation of the employment contract, which meant that employees were not protected against discriminatory conduct by their employers, including discriminatory firing, once they were on the job. Congress passed the Civil Rights Act of 1991, which served to strengthen the 1964 law by adding the rights for wronged employees to seek damages and to request a jury trial.

Under the Civil Rights Act of 1964, damages could be awarded if the employer could be shown to have intentionally discriminated against an employee because of race or ethnic background. An employee could not sue for damages because of discrimination based on gender, disability, or religion. Reinstatement and back pay were all that were available to individuals found to have been discriminated against because of sex, disability, or religion.

Under the Civil Rights Act of 1991, anyone claiming to have been the victim of intentional employment discrimination can sue for damages, although the law does set limits on the amount that can be awarded to individuals discriminated against because of sex, disability, or religion. The size of the employee workforce determines the maximum amount of damages that may be sought. The amounts range from $50,000 for an organization with up to 100 employees to $300,000 for institutions with 501 or more employees. Victims of discrimination based on race or national origin are not limited by law on the amount for which they may sue. Not only were the amounts raised by the new law, the Civil Rights Act of 1991 allowed employees suing for race or ethnic discrimination to request a jury trial. Those suing on sex, disability, or religious grounds are still not permitted jury trials. Those cases are heard by judges.

THE LAW IN BRIEF. Section 1981 of the Civil Rights Act of 1870. *ENACTED.* 1870. *SUMMARY.* Passed after the Civil War, the original intent was to give African-Americans "full and equal benefit of all laws . . . enjoyed by white people." Section 1981 relates to the right "to make and enforce contracts," including employment contracts. The courts interpreted the law to make discrimination in hiring and some promotional decisions illegal. The Civil Rights Act of 1991 made discrimination in all aspects of the employment relationship illegal. *COVERAGE.* Applies to all employers. *ENFORCEMENT.* Administered and enforced by the EEOC. *LAWSUITS.* Private lawsuits may be filed by individuals who are denied equal protection of the law and the right to enter into an employment contract. *REFERENCE.* Title 42, *U.S. Code*, sec. 1981.

THE LAW IN BRIEF. Title VII of the Civil Rights Act of 1964. As Amended by the Equal Employment Opportunity Act of 1972. *ENACTED.* 1964; major amendments 1972, 1991. *SUMMARY.* Title VII of this landmark act made it a violation of federal law for an employer to "fail or refuse to hire, to discharge any individual, or otherwise to discriminate against any individual with respect to compensation, terms, conditions, or privileges of employment because of the individual's race, color, religion, sex, or national origin; or to limit, segregate, or classify employees or applicants for employment in any way that would deprive, or tend to deprive, any individual of employment opportunities or otherwise adversely affect an individual's stature as an employee because of such individual's race, color, religion, sex, or national origin."[2] *COVERAGE.* Applies to employers with 15 or more workers. *ENFORCEMENT.* Administered and enforced by the EEOC. *CLAIMS.* Must be filed with the EEOC. *LAWSUITS.* Private lawsuits may be filed within 90 days of receipt of a right-to-sue notice from the EEOC or within 60 days of notification from the EEOC that it will not sue on the employee's behalf. *REFERENCE.* Title 42, *U.S. Code*, sec. 2000e.

THE LAW IN BRIEF. Civil Rights Act of 1991. *ENACTED.* 1991. *SUMMARY.* An amendment to Title VII of the Civil Rights Act of 1964, it makes employment discrimination laws applicable to all aspects of the employment relationship, and allows women, disabled individuals, and members of religious minorities to sue for damages for intentional discrimination and to choose trial by jury. *COVERAGE.* Applies to employers of 15 or more workers. *ENFORCEMENT.* Administered and enforced by the EEOC. *CLAIMS.* Must be filed with the EEOC within 180 days of the violation. *LAWSUITS.* Private lawsuits may be filed within 90 days of receipt of a right-to-sue notice from the EEOC. *REFERENCE.* Title 42, *U.S. Code*, sec. 12101 et seq.

THE LAW IN BRIEF. Executive Order 11246 (E.O. 11246). *EN-ACTED.* 1978. *SUMMARY.* Prohibits discrimination by federal contractors and subcontractors and requires that they have written affirmative action plans outlining the action they will take to hire and promote women and minorities. Employers found in violation of E.O. 11246 may have their federal contracts cancelled and future contracts denied. *COVERAGE.* Applies to all employers with contracts with the federal government in excess of $10,000. *ENFORCE-MENT.* Administered and enforced by the Office of Federal Contract Compliance Programs (OFCCP), a division of the Department of Labor. *CLAIMS.* Claims of violations are to be made to the OFCCP. Discrimination claims are to be made to the EEOC. *REFERENCE.* E.O. 11246.

Understanding Discrimination

Most employers are enlightened enough, after more than 30 years of exposure to significant antidiscrimination laws, to avoid such comments as, "Oh, we don't hire [fill in the name of a protected group] around here," or "We don't hire [fill in gender name] to do [fill in the name of a job] because [fill in the blank with any old antiquated stereotype]." Employers do run the risk, however, of unintentionally breaking the law through lack of understanding or failure to treat employees fairly.

Terms such as *disparate treatment, adverse impact, perpetuating discrimination, statistical imbalance,* and *reasonable accommodation* should be familiar to anyone who wishes to understand antidiscrimination laws. As will be seen in the following example, these items can play a major role in legal actions related to discrimination.

Let's suppose that Employee X is considering filing a discrimination lawsuit against his or her employer. In deciding whether or not to sue, Employee X is asking himself or herself three questions:

1. "Am I a member of a protected group because of my race, sex, religion, national origin, physical or mental disability, age, or sexual orientation?"

2. "Am I being treated differently from other employees who do the same or similar work?" If the answers to 1 and 2 are "yes," then:

3. "Is it because I'm black, female, over 40, disabled, or a member of any protected group?" If the answer is "yes" to all three questions, Employee X is probably checking out the yellow pages under "Attorney."

An attorney will advise Employee X that potential grounds for a suit are: disparate treatment; adverse impact; perpetuating discrimination; statistical imbalance; and/or reasonable accommodation.

If the employee believes that the employer treats him or her differently than other employees, the employee may sue for disparate treatment. For example, you are a woman and are paid less than a male counterpart who is performing essentially the same job. If you are getting paid less solely because you are a woman, that is disparate treatment. If the male is paid more because of seniority or a performance-based reason, the woman does not have a valid claim of disparate treatment.

If the employee or a group of employees believes the employer has a business policy or practice that affects the entire protected group differently than it affects members of other groups, the employee may sue based on adverse impact. An organization may have a policy or work rule that on its face is impartial, but a form of discrimination occurs when the rule falls more heavily on a protected group of workers than on other workers. For example, having a minimum height requirement has been found to adversely affect women and members of certain ethnic groups.

If the employer has a policy or practice that is a continuation of a policy or practice of past discrimination, the employee may sue the employer for perpetuating discrimination. For example, the practice of posting managerial opportunities in departments with only white employees or male employees may amount to discrimination if other employees have no other opportunities to learn about the job openings.

If the employer uses hiring or promotion practices that result in the hiring or promotion of fewer protected class members than other groups, the employee may sue the employer for creating a statistical imbalance. The employer may be guilty of discrimination if, for example, a certain interview process or other selection method creates a statistical imbalance in the workforce to the disadvantage of a protected group. The Civil Rights Act of 1991 requires the employer to show a business necessity for a practice leading to statistical imbalance rather than the less difficult proof of business justification under the Civil Rights Act of 1964.

Finally, if an employer fails to make reasonable accommodation for an employee with a disability, the employee may sue under the provisions of the ADA.

As an administrator, it is important to note that even though there is no longer (it is hoped) any blatant, clearly illegal racial discrimination by employers, there may exist policies, practices, or rules that limit unintentionally opportunities for protected groups and individuals. Those policies, practices, and rules need to be reviewed to ensure that they do not discriminate.

Ethnic Discrimination

The antidiscrimination laws specifically state that "all persons within the jurisdiction of the United States shall have the same right in every State and Territory to . . . the full and equal benefit of all laws for the security of persons and property as is enjoyed by white citizens." In addition, both federal and state laws prohibit race discrimination as well as discrimination against any ethnic minority. No intelligent employer will intentionally discriminate on the basis of race or ethnicity, but an employer may be found guilty of racial bias even if the employer doesn't actively participate in the practice. If the employer knew or should have known about a discriminatory practice, the employer may be found guilty. Any policy, practice, or rule that limits opportunities for minorities or has a disproportionate impact on minorities, even though unintentional, is in violation of the law.

Sex Discrimination

Discrimination based on sex occurs when an individual is treated differently because of his or her gender. Federal and state laws prohibit discrimination against anyone because of sex. An individual who is refused a job, a promotion, fired, or discriminated against in any terms or conditions of employment based on sex may have a discrimination claim. According to the EEOC, the employer may not do any of the following:

- Classify a job as "male" or "female"

- Advertise a job with a preference for "male" or "female"

- Refuse to hire married women

- Refuse to hire a woman because she is pregnant

- Refuse to hire an individual because he or she plans to have a family

- Refuse to hire an individual because he or she is or is not sterile

- Refuse to hire women of childbearing age for certain hazardous jobs

- Maintain separate career ladders for males and females

- Discriminate in promotions for males and females

- Maintain separate seniority lists for males and females

- Compensate males and females with different wages for the same work done under the same or similar working conditions

- Deny health insurance based on sex

- Offer different health insurance plans to males and females

- Treat pregnancy differently than any other disability

- Deny participation in pension or retirement plans based on sex

- Offer different retirement plans to males and females

- Offer different vacation benefits to males and females

- Offer different holiday benefits to males and females

- Offer different fringe benefits to males and females

The one area where an employer may specify a preference for a male or female is a bona fide occupation qualification (BFOQ), where the employer can demonstrate that being a male or being a female is crucial to the position. For example, hiring male security guards for an all-male prison or considering only female applicants for an acting role as Cleopatra constitute BFOQs. The common theme in all of the prohibitions is that, with the exception of the bona fide occupational qualification, the employer cannot treat males and females differently when it comes to employment matters.

Sexual Harassment

Guidelines issued by the EEOC define sexual harassment as unwelcome sexual advances, requests for sexual favors, and other verbal or physical conduct of a sexual nature occurring under any of the following three conditions:

1. Where submission is either explicitly or implicitly a term or condition of employment;

2. Where submission or rejection of the conduct forms the basis for an employment action; or

3. Where the conduct has either the purpose or effect of substantially interfering with the individual's work performance or creating an intimidating, hostile, or offensive working environment.

Policies created in compliance with the guidelines govern how libraries deal with sexual harassment complaints. Those policies must encourage victims to report sexual harassment, offer several avenues for reporting objectionable conduct, offer speedy investigation of complaints, discipline violators, and protect persons who report sexual harassment from retaliation. It is important to note that the employer is liable for sexual harassment by employees even if the employer is unaware of the conduct and the institution has a policy prohibiting sexual harassment. It is important that action be taken on complaints.

Sexual Orientation

Federal court decisions have served to declare that Title VII of the Civil Rights Act of 1964 protects job applicants and employees from discrimination based on sexual orientation, but there is no federal law specifically addressing the issue. Sexual orientation relates to an individual's preference for heterosexuality, homosexuality, bisexuality, or identification with one of these preferences. Sexual orientation may also be referred to as lifestyle.

Eight states have comprehensive nondiscrimination laws and more than 25 cities and 100 counties in the United States have legalized ordinances and policies banning discrimination based on sexual orientation since the widespread attention given to Anita Bryant's campaign to repeal a Dade County, Florida, gay rights ordinance in 1977. Cities and counties across the United States have either decided to include sexual orientation in their antidiscrimination statutes or have repealed such ordinances. Fully one-fifth of the American population is covered by such ordinances or policies as of mid-1993. The ordinances differ greatly from one locale to another, but they typically amend the human rights or antidiscrimination statute by adding "sexual orientation" to the list of protected categories. Most of the ordinances and policies are found in large cities with virtually none in smaller communities. Employee protections on the basis of sexual orientation or individual lifestyle are afforded only to those in communities with ordinances.

As an example of an organization's stand on the issue, the American Library Association's (ALA) antidiscrimination policy (54.3) states, "ALA is committed to equality of opportunity for all library employees or applicants for employment, regardless of race, color, creed, sex, age, or physical or mental handicap, individual lifestyle or national origin."[3] By advertising through ALA services, libraries and other organizations agree to comply with the policy. Direct or implied biases are edited out of ads placed in ALA publications.

Recent controversies surrounding gays in the military and discrimination against gays in federal hiring demonstrate that the issue of discrimination based on sexual orientation remains to be solved.

Disabled Workers

The Vocational Rehabilitation Act of 1973 was passed by Congress to protect the employment rights of disabled workers. That act applied to only federal contractors and subcontractors. The ADA, which took effect in 1992, extends coverage to all employers of 15 or more workers. A disabled individual, for the purposes of the law, is a person who has a physical or mental impairment that limits one or more major life activities, has a record of such impairment, or is regarded by others as having such an impairment. Impairments that limit major life activities must be substantial as opposed to minor and include impairments that limit seeing, hearing, speaking, walking, breathing, performing manual tasks, learning, caring for oneself, and working. An individual with paralysis, substantial hearing or visual impairment, mental retardation, or a learning disability would be covered, but an individual with a minor, nonchronic condition of short duration such as a sprain, broken bone, or infection would normally not be covered. A person with a history of cancer or of mental illness would be covered. The third part of the definition protects individuals who are regarded and treated as though they have a substantially limiting disability; for example, the law would protect an individual who is disfigured from adverse employment decisions because the employer feared negative reactions from co-workers. AIDS victims are included in the latter definition as well.

The basic provision of the ADA prohibits discrimination against qualified disabled persons by requiring that the employer make reasonable accommodation for those who can perform the job unless that accommodation would create an undue hardship for the employer. To be a qualified disabled person, the individual must have an impairment that limits one of the major life activities needed to be able to perform the essential functions of the job. The sole fact that an individual is disabled can't eliminate the individual from consideration. Reasonable accommodation requires that the employer modify the job application process so disabled persons can apply in the first place and adjust the work environment in such a way that the disabled individual can perform the job. It should be noted here that the employer may make preemployment inquiries into the ability of a job applicant to perform job-related functions. However, an employer cannot ask whether the applicant is an individual with a disability.

A reasonable accommodation might include altering the structure of the work area to make it accessible, acquiring new equipment, modifying work schedules, or simply putting a desk on blocks to accommodate a wheelchair. An accommodation does not have to be made if it would create an "undue hardship." An undue hardship on an employer depends in large part on the type and cost of the accommodation needed, the size of the organization, and the size of the budget. A large organization would have to go to greater lengths than a small business to make a reasonable accommodation. An accommodation could also be considered an undue hardship if it would unduly disrupt other employees or customers, but not if the disruption is caused simply by fear or prejudice. Even in the case of undue hardship, an employer may be required to provide an alternative accommodation.

The ADA excludes from coverage applicants and employees who are currently using drugs illegally, but does not exclude individuals who have been successfully rehabilitated. ADA calls largely for commonsense solutions to making accommodations for disabled workers who, with the accommodation, can perform the essential functions of the job. A larger, more difficult problem revolves around those few individuals who would take advantage of a disability to find a way to sue.

THE LAW IN BRIEF. Vocational Rehabilitation Act of 1973 (Rehab Act) *ENACTED.* 1973. *SUMMARY.* This legislation extended Title VII antidiscrimination protections to disabled individuals. The act prohibits discrimination in employment on the basis of a mental or physical disability. The act defines a disabled person as one who "has a physical or mental impairment which substantially limits one or more of life's major activities, has a record of such impairment, and is regarded as having such an impairment." *COVERAGE.* Applies to federal contractors and subcontractors. *EXCEPTIONS.* Does not apply to those workers who use illegal drugs or who use alcohol to an extent that its use prevents them from performing the job. *ENFORCEMENT.* Administered and enforced by the OFCCP, a division of the Department of Labor. *CLAIMS.* Claims of violations are to be made to the OFCCP. Discrimination claims are to be made to the EEOC. *LAWSUITS.* Private lawsuits may be filed within 90 days of receipt of a right-to-sue notice from the EEOC or within 60 days of notification from the EEOC that it will not sue on the employee's behalf. *REFERENCE.* Title 29, *U.S. Code*, sec. 701 et seq.

THE LAW IN BRIEF. Americans with Disabilities Act (ADA). *ENACTED.* 1990. *SUMMARY.* Prohibits discrimination against qualified disabled workers in hiring, compensation, and other terms and conditions of employment. Requires employers to make reasonable accommodations for individuals who are otherwise qualified to perform the essential functions of the job as long as those accommodations would not be an undue hardship on the employer. Applies specifically to victims of AIDS. *COVERAGE.* Applies to employers of 15 or more workers. *EXCEPTIONS.* Does not protect employees or applicants who are using drugs illegally. *ENFORCEMENT*. Administered and enforced by the EEOC. *CLAIMS*. Must be filed with the EEOC within 180 days of the violation. *LAWSUITS*. Private lawsuits may be filed within 90 days of receipt of a right-to-sue notice from the EEOC. *REFERENCE*. Title 42, *U.S. Code*, sec. 12101 et seq.

Age Discrimination

The ADEA protects employees from discrimination because of age. Workers over the age of 40 are protected by the ADEA, and state laws have been passed to extend that protection in many cases. The law forbids employers from specifying any age preference in job ads except minimum age requirements, for example, for an individual who will serve alcoholic beverages. Employers can't refuse to hire, pay employees less, or discriminate in any way because of age. Courts recognize four elements necessary for a prima facie case for age discrimination:

1. The individual is in the protected age group—over 40 under the ADEA or younger for some states.

2. The individual was terminated, not promoted, or was the object of an adverse employment decision.

3. The individual was qualified for the position.

4. The adverse decision was made under circumstances that give rise to an inference of age discrimination.

In 1989, the Supreme Court ruled that the ADEA did not apply to employee benefit plans; however, in 1990, Congress passed the Older Workers Benefit Protection Act (OWBPA), which extended age discrimination prohibitions to benefits. The Act states that if an employer has an employee benefit plan, the employer has to expend the same amount of money for the older worker's benefits as for the younger worker, even though the resulting coverage may be less; for health insurance coverage, premiums and benefits must be equal.

THE LAW IN BRIEF. Age Discrimination in Employment Act (ADEA). *ENACTED*. 1967. Amended by additional law, including the OWBPA of 1990. *SUMMARY*. Prohibits discrimination against workers who are between the ages of 40 and 70 on the basis of age. *COVERAGE*. Applies to employers of 20 or more workers. *EXCEPTIONS*. Does not apply in cases where age is a BFOQ of the job. *ENFORCEMENT*. Administered and enforced by the EEOC.

CLAIMS. Must be filed with the EEOC within 180 days of the violation. *LAWSUITS*. Private lawsuits may be filed within 90 days of receipt of a right-to-sue notice from the EEOC or within 60 days of notification from the EEOC that it will not sue on the employee's behalf. *STATE LAW*. Some states have laws that prohibit discrimination against workers under age 40 and over age 70. *REFERENCE*. Title 29, *U.S. Code*, sec. 621.

National Origin Discrimination

The only question an employer can ask a prospective employee related to country of origin is whether or not the applicant is authorized to work in the United States. Once hired, the individual must comply with the provisions of the Immigration Reform and Control Act (IRCA), under which the employer and employee complete applicable sections of the INS I-9 form. Under federal law, employees cannot be discriminated against because of place of origin or because employees have physical, cultural, or linguistic characteristics of a certain nationality. Simply put, employees are protected from employment discrimination because they "look foreign" or have a foreign accent.

The prohibitions against harassment on the basis of national origin are the same as those for sexual harassment. Title VII of the Civil Rights Act of 1964 protects workers against ethnic slurs or conduct that serves to create a hostile working environment.

THE LAW IN BRIEF. Immigration Reform and Control Act (IRCA). *ENACTED*. 1986. *SUMMARY*. Makes it illegal to recruit, hire, or refer for hire any unauthorized alien; requires documentation of identity and eligibility of workers to work in the United States; and prohibits discrimination on the basis of national origin or citizenship status. Employer and employee complete applicable sections of the INS I-9 form. *COVERAGE*. Applies to all employers. *EXCEPTIONS*. Does not apply to employees hired prior to November 6, 1986. The antidiscrimination provisions of the IRCA do not apply to employers with fewer than four employees. *ENFORCEMENT*. Administered and enforced by the Immigration and Naturalization Service and the Department of Justice. *CLAIMS*. Must be filed with the Department of Justice or the EEOC. *LAWSUITS*. Private lawsuits may be filed within 90 days of receipt of a right-to-sue notice from the EEOC or within 60 days of notification from the EEOC that it will not sue on the employee's behalf. *REFERENCE*. Title 8, *U.S. Code*, sec. 1324.

Religious Discrimination

Individuals are protected from discrimination based on religion by the First Amendment of the U.S. Constitution. The overriding concern in employment is that all individuals be treated equally, whether equally good or equally bad. Inasmuch as more than 70 percent of the employees in an organization are likely to fall into one of the protected groups discussed in this chapter, the minority are, in effect, the majority. Thus it simply makes sense to treat all employees equally.

References

1. *Patterson v. McLean Credit Union*, 109 Supreme Court 2363 (1989).

2. *Civil Rights Act of 1964* (PL 88-352, 2 July 1964), 78 *United States Statutes at Large:* 255.

3. "Career Leads: ALA Guidelines," *American Libraries* 26, no. 8 (September 1995): 832. ALA's guidelines appear each month in the classified advertisements section of *American Libraries*.

Bibliography

Aggarwal, Arjun Prakash. *Sex Discrimination: Employment Law and Practices*. Clearwater, Fla.: Butterworths, 1994.

AIDS, the New Workplace Issues. New York: American Management Association, 1988.

Anderson, Howard J. *Major Employment Law Principles Established by the EEOC, the OFCCP and the Courts*. Washington, D.C.: Bureau of National Affairs, 1980.

Andiappan, P., M. Reavley, and S. Silver. "Discrimination Against Pregnant Employees: An Analysis of Arbitration and Human Rights Tribunal Decisions in Canada." *Journal of Business Ethics* 9, no. 2 (February 1990): 143.

Beck-Dudley, Caryn, and Glenn M. McEvoy. "Performance Appraisals and Discrimination Suits: Do Courts Pay Attention to Validity?" *Employee Responsibilities and Rights Journal* 4, no. 2 (June 1991): 149.

Bloch, Farrell E. *Antidiscrimination Law and Minority Employment: Recruitment Practices and Regulatory Constraints*. Chicago: University of Chicago Press, 1994.

Bogas, Kathleen L. "Discrimination Cases: What to Expect." *Trial* 27, no. 6 (June 1991): 41.

Brown, Kathleen C., and Joan G. Turner. *AIDS: Policies and Programs for the Workplace*. New York: Van Nostrand Reinhold, 1989.

Burns James A., Jr. "Sexual Harassment: Is It Always 'Unwelcome'?" *Employee Relations Law Journal* 18, no. 4 (Spring 1993): 681.

Button, James W., et al. "Where Local Laws Prohibit Discrimination Based on Sexual Orientation." *Public Management* 77, no. 4 (April 1995): 9-12.

The Civil Rights Act of 1991: Its Impact on Employment Discrimination Litigation. New York: Practising Law Institute, 1992.

Coleman, Francis T. "Creating a Workplace Free of Sexual Harassment." *Association Management* 45, no. 2 (February 1993): 69.

Conte, Alba. "State Remedies for Sexual Harassment at Work." *Trial* 29, no. 11 (November 1993): 56.

Crow, Stephen M. "The Civil Rights Act of 1991: Death Knell for Traditional Faculty Staffing and Pay Practices in Business Schools?" *Employee Responsibilities and Rights Journal* 7, no. 3 (September 1994): 247.

―――. "Excessive Absenteeism and the Americans with Disabilities Act." *The Arbitration Journal* 48, no.1 (March 1993): 65.

Dworkin, Terry Morehead. "Harassment in the 1990s." *Business Horizons* 36, no. 2 (March 1993): 52.

Egler, Theresa Donahue. "Legal Trends: Five Myths About Sexual Harassment." *HrMagazine: On Human Resource Management* 40, no. 1 (January 1995): 27.

Elliott, Robert H., and Thomas M. Wilson. "AIDS in the Workplace: Public Personnel Management and the Law." *Public Personnel Management* 16, no. 3 (fall 1987): 209.

Foos, Donald D., and Nancy C. Pack, eds. *How Libraries Must Comply with the Americans with Disabilities Act*. Phoenix, Ariz.: Oryx, 1992.

Gilchrist, Michelle. "How to Deal with the Problem of Sexual Harassment." *Business Review Weekly* 14, no. 33 (August 1992): 70.

Gold, Michael Evan. *An Introduction to the Law of Employment Discrimination*. Ithaca, N.Y.: ILR Press, 1993.

Goldberg, Janet E. "Employees with Mental and Emotional Problems—Workplace Security and Implications of State Discrimination Laws, the Americans with Disabilities Act, the Rehabilitation Act, Workers Compensation, and Related Issues." *Stetson Law Review* 24, no. 1 (fall 1994): 201.

Gutek, Barbara. "Sexual Harassment: Rights and Responsibilities." *Employee Responsibilities and Rights Journal* 6, no. 4 (December 1993): 325.

Hames, David S. "Disciplining Sexual Harassers: What's Fair?" *Employee Responsibilities and Rights Journal* 7, no. 3 (September 1994): 207.

Hartman, Laura. "The Disabled Employee and Reasonable Accommodation Under the Minnesota Human Rights Act: Where Does Absenteeism Attributable to the Disability Fit into the Law?" *William Mitchell Law Review* 19, no. 4 (fall 1993): 905.

"Illegal Aliens and Workers Compensation: The Aftermath of Sure-Tan and IRCA." *Hofstra Labor Law Journal* 7, no. 2 (spring 1990): 393.

Johnson, James A., ed. *AIDS in the Workplace: A Policy Development and Resource Guide for Human Service Organizations.* Memphis, Tenn.: Shelby House, 1989.

Larson, Lex K. *Civil Rights Act of 1991.* New York: Matthew Bender, 1992.

Lindemann, Barbara, and David D. Kadue. *Sexual Harassment in Employment Law.* Washington, D.C.: Bureau of National Affairs, 1992.

Mook, Jonathan R., ed. *Americans with Disabilities Act: Employee Rights & Employer Obligations.* New York: Matthew Bender, 1992.

Nager, Glen D., and Edward K.M. Bilich. "The Civil Rights Act of 1991 Going Forward." *Employee Relations Law Journal* 20, no. 2 (fall 1994): 237.

Parliman, Gregory C., and Rosalie J. Shoeman. "National Origin Discrimination or Employer Prerogative? An Analysis of Language Rights in the Workplace." *Employee Relations Law Journal* 19, no. 4 (spring 1994): 551.

Paul, Niall A. "The Civil Rights Act of 1991: What Does It Really Accomplish?" *Employee Relations Law Journal* 17, no. 4 (spring 1992): 567.

Perritt, Henry H. *Civil Rights Act of 1991: Special Report.* New York: Wiley Law Publications, 1992.

Religious Accommodation in the Workplace: A Legal and Practical Handbook. Washington, D.C.: Bureau of National Affairs, 1987.

Richey, Charles R. *Manual on Employment Discrimination Law and Civil Rights Actions in the Federal Courts,* 2nd ed. Deerfield, Ill.: Clark Boardman Callaghan, 1994.

"The Rights of the Pregnant Employee." *Small Business Report* 15, no. 5 (May 1990): 64.

Sepanik, Jani. *Drug Testing, Sexual Harassment, Smoking: Employee Rights Issues.* Washington, D.C.: Management Information Service, 1988.

Simon, Howard A., and Erin Daly. "Sexual Orientation and Workplace Rights: A Potential Land Mine for Employers?" *Employee Relations Law Journal* 18, no. 1 (summer 1992): 29.

Smith, James Monroe. "The Legal Rights of People with HIV/AIDS." *EAP Digest* 13, no. 5 (July 1993): 30.

Steiner, Alison. "The Americans with Disabilities Act of 1990 and Workers Compensation: The Employees' Perspective." *Mississippi Law Journal* 62, no. 3 (spring 1993): 631.

Stewart, Alva W. *Privacy in the Workplace: A Bibliographic Survey.* Monticello, Ill.: Vance Bibliographies, [1987].

Susser, Peter A. "The ADA: Dramatically Expanded Federal Rights for Disabled Americans." *Employee Relations Law Journal* 16, no. 2 (fall 1990): 157.

Turner, Ronald. "The Past and Future of Affirmative Action: A Guide and Analysis for Human Resource Professionals and Corporate Counsel." *Employee Responsibilities and Rights Journal* 5, no. 4 (December 1992): 379.

Wahl, Edward T., and Jenny B. Wahl. "Disability Discrimination and Workers Compensation After the Americans with Disabilities Act: Sorting out the Rights and Duties." *Hamline Law Review* 16, no. 1 (fall 1992): 81.

Walworth, Carla R., Lisa J. Damon, and Carole F. Wilder. "Walking a Fine Line: Managing the Conflicting Obligations of the Americans with Disabilities Act and Workers' Compensation Laws." *Employee Relations Law Journal* 19, no. 2 (fall 1993): 221.

Waxman, Merle. "Constructive Responses to Sexual Harassment in the Workplace." *Employee Responsibilities and Rights Journal* 7, no. 3 (September 1994): 243.

Wyld, David C., and Sam D. Cappel. "Believing in Employment Discrimination: The Case of Forrest Mims, Scientific American, and Title VII Protection." *Employee Responsibilities and Rights Journal* 5, no. 1 (March 1992): 1.

■■■■■■■ Chapter Seven

Health, Safety, and Privacy

The brain is a wonderful organ;
it starts working the moment you
get up in the morning and does not
stop until you get into the office.
Robert Frost (1874-1963)

As this is written, there is concern about how far the government has gone and should go in ensuring the health, safety, and privacy of employees in the workplace. Some businesses are concerned that the government is imposing too many regulations, has too many reporting requirements, and is punishing too harshly for violations. Others would argue that the government has a role in ensuring that employees are safe in the work environment because employees would otherwise be at risk. Likewise, the organization has a responsibility to maintain the privacy of personnel records.

Occupational Safety and Health Act

The Bureau of Labor Statistics reports that in 1992, 6.8 million workplace injuries and illnesses occurred in the United States.[1] However alarming those numbers, they were worse prior to enactment of the Occupational Safety and Health Act (OSHA) in 1970. Prior to 1970, states enacted their own workplace health and safety laws, which were often not well enforced. The act established some basic workplace rules and an enforcement procedure that includes the employees' ability to report suspected violations.

The OSHA requires that employers comply with a general safety standard, which applies to all workplaces, and a specific safety standard, which applies to conditions in specific work environments. The general safety standard states that employers have "a general duty to provide a workplace that is free from 'recognized hazards' that are likely to cause death or severe physical harm." Conditions or situations that are obviously dangerous, that the employer knows about, or that are considered hazardous in a specific industry are "recognized hazards."[2]

Safety and Health Standards

The OSHA has established safety and health standards covering virtually all conceivable aspects of the workplace. Some of those specific safety standards include:

- Providing control of ventilation, temperature, and noise levels

- Assuring that the workplace is clean and orderly, and that the entrances, exits, and stairways are clear of obstructions

- Making sure that there are adequate emergency exits, fire protections and alarm systems, sprinklers, and evacuation plans

- Having medical and first aid treatment available

- Providing personal protective equipment for eyes, face, head, feet, and respiratory systems where needed

- Covering general working conditions, including such things as waste disposal, water, toilets, and lighting

Specific Working Conditions

Employers are required to keep the workplace clean and in an orderly condition. Rest rooms and drinking fountains are to be cleaned regularly, and floors should be swept and cleaned regularly. The workplace must have water that is suitable for drinking and washing. Separate toilets must be maintained for males and females, the number of which are as follows:

Number of Employees	Number of Toilets
1-15	1
16-35	2
36-55	3
56-80	4
81-110	5
111-150	6
more than 150	1 more for each additional 40 employees

An exception to the rule on separate toilets is rest rooms that can be locked from the inside and used by one person at a time. Hot and cold water must be available in all rest rooms. Eating is not allowed in rest rooms or where food would be exposed to hazardous chemicals.

Temperatures in the workplace are to be kept at a comfortable level to avoid extremes that would affect worker health or safety. Employees may not be exposed to constant noise. When noise levels are above 85 decibels for more than eight hours, employees are to be provided with ear protection. Lights should be adequate to prevent eyestrain and angled to reduce glare. Smoking is not permitted in elevators. Although not directly because of the OSHA, smoking is prohibited nearly everywhere.

The OSHA also covers medical and first aid. There must be medical care available within a reasonable distance, or, if not, there should be someone on hand who is trained to give first aid. If employees are working with potentially dangerous chemicals, such as in the library's conservation lab, the law requires that the workplace be equipped with suitable facilities for immediate flushing of the eyes and body. Fire extinguishers must be available according to specific OSHA requirements depending on the type of potential fire, and if the building is big enough, it must be equipped with fire alarms.

OSHA Inspections

The law provides that OSHA inspectors can enter and inspect the workplace with or without advance notice to determine compliance. Most visits are made as the result of an employee complaint. The inspectors may check organization records, review compliance with the federal hazard communication standard, review fire protection measures, and/or review the organization's general health and safety plan. Random, unannounced inspections are done more often in the more hazardous industries such as construction or manufacturing.

OSHA Reporting Requirements

The primary reports an employer of more than 10 workers has to keep as specified by the OSHA are the following:

Log and Summary of Injuries and Illnesses (OSHA Form No. 100). The log has to include those injuries or illnesses that result in a fatality, lost days of work, transfer of an individual to another job, termination of employment, medical treatment, unconsciousness, or restriction of work or motion. Injuries are to be reported within six days. Form 100 must be retained for at least five years.

Annual Summary of Injuries and Illnesses (OSHA Form No. 200). By February 1 of each year, the employer must post an annual summary of injuries and illnesses. The summary must remain posted until at least March 1 and must include the year's total number of occupational injuries and illnesses, the calendar year covered, the organization's name and address, the signature and title of the person signing the form, and the date.

Records of Occupational Injury or Illness (OSHA Form No. 101). A record of each occupational injury or illness must be kept and must include the following: employer's name and address; the injured or sick employee's name, social security number, address, sex, age, occupation, and department; details of the accident, including the place and how it happened; a description of the injury or illness; the date it occurred; the name and address of the doctor and hospital if applicable; and the name and title of the person completing the report. Form 101 must be retained for at least five years.

Report of the Fatality or Hospitalization of Five or More Workers. All employers are required to report to the OSHA area director, within 48 hours, any accident resulting in a fatality or serious injury to five or more workers. The report shall include the circumstances of the accident, the number of fatalities, and the extent of injuries to other employees.

Medical Records. The OSHA requires employers to keep employees' medical records for at least 30 years after their termination of employment.

The OSHA requires employers to post OSHA notices informing employees about the Act. Included are the OSHA "Job Safety & Health" poster, OSHA Form No. 200, and copies of any OSHA citations for violations.

Right-to-Know Laws

If the employer uses, produces, or distributes hazardous chemicals, the OSHA requires that the employer develop a written hazard communication plan. The plan must list the hazardous chemicals used in the workplace; describe the chemicals; describe how the employer will comply with the OSHA's hazardous communication standard, which gives employees the right to know about the dangers those chemicals could pose; and describe compliance with the OSHA labeling requirements, Material Safety Data Sheet (MSDS) information requirements, and training requirements.

MSDSs, which list the chemical's properties and dangers, proper handling techniques, and appropriate medical treatment in case of exposure, must be provided by manufacturers. If provided to the employer, the MSDSs must be provided to the employees exposed to the chemicals. Manufacturers of chemicals must also label chemicals in a way that identifies the trade and common names of the chemical, warns of potential hazards, and identifies the manufacturer. Organizations receiving these chemicals must make sure the labels remain intact.

Employers are required to give employees access to records of exposure to toxic substances and harmful agents within 15 days of the employee request. Records of such exposures are to be kept for 30 years. Employers are also required to provide training on the handling of any hazardous chemical introduced into the work area. Employers must inform employees about any chemicals, toxic substances, or other substances in the workplace that may cause birth defects or constitute a hazard to an individual's reproductive system or fetus when exposed on the job.[3] Lastly, all employers must inform employees about their rights under the hazard communication law, either by posting a notice or by informing employees in person. This information must be given when requested by an employee in writing, within a month of hiring, or within a month of transferring an employee into an area that involves exposure to hazardous chemicals. Employers may not discriminate against, discipline, or discharge employees for exercising their "right-to-know" rights.

Employee Complaints and Whistle-Blower Protection

If employees think that the employer is violating health and safety laws, they may file confidential complaints with the Occupational Safety and Health Administration within 30 days of the alleged violation. An employee who has filed an OSHA complaint is protected by the OSHA against discrimination, discipline, or discharge.

The OSHA also protects employees from retaliation for refusing to work on jobs they legitimately believe are unsafe. But that doesn't mean that employees can simply walk off the job. Certain conditions must first be met. The unsafe condition must be one that presents a substantial risk of death, disease, or serious physical harm, a risk that a reasonable person would recognize. Also, the condition must result from the employer's violation of safety and health standards. The situation must be so urgent that there isn't enough time to eliminate the risk and, when asked to correct the problem, the employer couldn't or wouldn't. If an employee refuses to work in a condition considered unsafe, he or she can be reassigned until an investigation is completed and the situation rectified if possible. If after a satisfactory investigation, the employer believes the complaint is unwarranted, the employee *can* be required to return to work. The employee may still elect to file a confidential complaint with the Occupational Safety and Health Administration, which will be investigated by that agency.

OSHA Violations and Penalties

The Occupational Safety and Health Administration may issue citations to employers for varying degrees of violations. The following are the types of violations and penalties:

- *De minimis* violations: minor violations—No penalty

- Nonserious violations: conditions not likely to cause serious harm—maximum fine: $7,000

- Serious violations: violations resulting in probability of serious injury or death—maximum fine: $7,000

- Willful violations: deliberate or intentional violations—maximum fine: $70,000

- Repeated violations: subsequent occurrence of a violation within three years—maximum fine: $70,000

THE LAW IN BRIEF. Occupational Safety and Health Act (OSHA). ENACTED. 1970. SUMMARY. Enacted to ensure safe and healthful working conditions for every worker in the United States. Provisions of the act: to create public safety and health standards; to conduct inspections and investigations; to issue citations and propose penalties; and to require employers to keep records of job-related injuries and illnes
ses. *COVERAGE.* Applies to all employers engaged in interstate commerce, regardless of the number of employees. *ENFORCEMENT.* Administered and enforced by the Occupational Safety and Health Administration. *CLAIMS.* Must be filed with the administration, which can conduct inspections of workplaces with or without complaints being filed. *LAWSUITS.* An employer may be fined up to $1,000 a day for failing to correct a problem, up to $7,000 for a serious violation, and up to $70,000 for a willful violation. *STATE LAW.* Some states have health and safety laws that are approved by the administration. *REFERENCE. Title 29, U.S. Code, sec. 651 et seq.*

Smoking as a Health and Safety Issue

Although there are no federal laws prohibiting smoking in the workplace, there are a number of states with laws prohibiting smoking in certain places. Most universities prohibit smoking in all but designated areas—libraries seldom provide smoking areas. Various studies have shown that smokers have more health problems, more absenteeism, higher mortality rates, and higher accident rates. Employers have also been successfully sued by nonsmokers who have been exposed to secondhand smoke on the job. In one instance, an employee successfully sued the employer, claiming he was permanently sensitized to secondhand smoke as a result of being forced to work near heavy smokers.[4] Another employee claimed to be disabled under the Vocational Rehabilitation Act of 1973 because his sensitivity to smoke limited one of his major life activities. His employer was required to move him away from smokers.[5] More and more employers are simply prohibiting smoking in the workplace.

Personnel Files

The files in the library's human resources office are often the subject of speculation by library employees because they do not know what those files contain. Much of the information consists simply of records the employer is required to keep, either in the library's personnel files or the university's human resources office. Those records include payroll records, time sheets, tax information, sick leave records, annual leave records, workers compensation records, health insurance forms, and retirement information. Records of personnel action, including change of address, change of name, promotions, and salary increases, are all part of the file.

Any information in an employee's personnel file other than that required by various government agencies should be strictly job-related. Employee personnel files include information relating to hiring, promotion, disciplinary action, and salary history. There should be nothing in the file that has not also been provided to the employee. Copies of performance appraisals or any documentation relating to performance must have also been given to the employee in order to be placed in the file. The employee may be asked, for the purposes of the organization's affirmative action plan, if he or she wishes to self-identify as a female, minority, and/or veteran. The information cannot be used for any other purpose and should not be included in the individual's personnel file.

Access to Personnel Files

Generally, state laws govern the availability of personnel files. Many states allow employees to review their own personnel files at reasonable intervals, such as once or twice a year. Usually the inspection of a personnel file must be done in the presence of a personnel staff person. In other states, the employer may require that a request to view the file be made in writing.

There may be information in an employee's personnel file that should not be shown to the employee and that should be removed before the employee sees the file. Examples include information being gathered as part of a criminal investigation, letters of reference, and any other information that, if shown to the employee, would violate another individual's right to privacy. Additionally, the confidentiality of medical records is covered by the Americans with Disabilities Act (ADA). Medical records must be kept on separate forms and in a file separate from personnel records. The only people who may have access to them are a manager or supervisor who needs to be informed if the employee has a disability that needs to be accommodated; first aid or medical personnel, in case of an emergency; and government officials doing an ADA compliance review.

Access to personnel files is usually restricted to the employee and to those with a need to know, generally the individual's supervisor and the library administration. Most states have laws that expressly allow the employee to request that dated or erroneous information be removed from the personnel file and, failing that, to insert an explanation of any document with which the employee disagrees. To ensure confidentiality, all personnel files should be kept locked.

References

1. "Occupational Injuries and Illnesses: Counts, Rates, and Characteristics, 1992," *U.S. Department of Labor*, April 1995: 1.

2. *Occupational Safety and Health Act of 1970* (PL 91-596, 29 Dec. 1970), 84 *United States Statutes at Large:* 1593.

3. Even though the employer must inform employees about potential dangers, the U.S. Supreme Court has held that fetal protection rules that ban pregnant or childbearing-age women from working on jobs that may cause birth defects are sexually biased and therefore illegal.

4. *Kuhahl v. Wisconsin Bell Co.,* Wisconsin Labor and Industrial Review Committee, No. 88-000676 (1990).

5. *Vickers v. Veterans Administration,* U.S. District Court, Western Washington, 549 Fed. Supp. (1982).

Bibliography

Babcock, Michael W. "The Role of the Federal Employers' Liability Act in Railroad Safety." *Workers Compensation Law Review* 15 (1992): 531.

Berenbeim, Ronald. *Employee Privacy*. New York: The Conference Board, 1990.

Bible, Jon D., and Darien A. McWhirter. *Privacy in the Workplace: A Guide for Human Resource Managers*. New York: Quorum Books, 1990.

Britt, Phillip. "Occupational Safety." *Safety & Health* 150, no. 4 (October 1994): 68.

Cheavens, Joseph D. "Terminal Worker Injury and Death Claims." *Workers Compensation Law Review* 13 (1990): 375.

Cornish, Craig M. *Drugs and Alcohol in the Workplace: Testing and Privacy*. Wilmette, Ill.: Callaghan, 1988.

Etter, Irvin B. "Ergonomics: Don't Wait for OSHA." *Safety & Health* 151, no. 2 (February 1995): 3.

Force, Robert, and Xia Chen. "An Introduction to Personal Injury and Death Claims in the People's Republic of China." *Workers Compensation Law Review* 15 (1992): 29.

Gordon, Brett R. "Employee Involvement in the Enforcement of the Occupational Safety and Health Laws of Canada and the United States." *Comparative Labor Law Journal* 15, no. 4 (summer 1994): 527.

Hasty, Keith N. "Worker's Compensation: Will College and University Professors Be Compensated for Mental Injuries Caused by Work-Related Stress?" *The Journal of College and University Law* 17, no. 4 (spring 1991): 535.

Kohn, Stephen M., and Michael D. Kohn. *The Labor Lawyer's Guide to the Rights and Responsibilities of Employee Whistleblowers*. New York: Quorum Books, 1988.

Kramer, Andrew M., and Laurie F. Calder. "The Emergence of Employees' Privacy Rights: Smoking and the Workplace." *The Labor Lawyer* 8, no. 2 (spring 1992): 313.

Kuzmits, Frank E. "Workplace Homicide: Prediction or Prevention?" *S.A.M. Advanced Management Journal* 57, no. 2 (spring 1992): 4.

Mathews, Nell E. "The Interplay Between Employment Law and the Workers Compensation Act: Termination, Obstruction of Benefits, and Accommodation of the Injured Worker." *Hennepin Lawyer* 63, no. 3 (January 1994): 4.

OSHA: Employee Workplace Rights 1994. Washington, D.C.: U.S. Department of Labor, Occupational Safety and Health Administration, 1994.

"OSHA Targets Recordkeeping Violations." *Occupational Health & Safety* 64, no. 1 (January 1995): 36.

"The Right to Know." *The Engineer* 276, no. 7137 (February 1993): 20.

Rinefort, Foster C., and David D. Van Fleet. "Safety Issues Beyond the Workplace: Estimated Relationships Between Work Injuries and Available Supervision." *Employee Responsibilities and Rights Journal* 6, no. 1 (March 1993): 1.

Scowcroft, Jerome C. "Longshore and Harbor Workers Compensation Act—Railroad Employees: The LHWCA Covers Railroad Employees Injured While Performing Work Integral to Loading or Unloading a Ship." *Journal of Maritime Law and Commerce* 22, no. 2 (April 1991): 309.

Sepanik, Jani. *Drug Testing, Sexual Harassment, Smoking: Employee Rights Issues*. Washington, D.C.: Management Information Service, 1988.

Shepard, Ira Michael. *Workplace Privacy: Employee Testing, Surveillance, Wrongful Discharge, and Other Areas of Vulnerability*, 2nd ed. Washington, D.C.: Bureau of National Affairs, 1989.

Thorne, Thomas W., Jr. "The Impact of the Longshore and Harbor Workers Compensation Act on Third Party Litigation." *Tulane Law Review* 68, no. 2/3 (January 1994): 557.

Warner, Daniel M. "'We Do Not Hire Smokers': May Employers Discriminate Against Smokers?" *Employee Responsibilities and Rights Journal* 7, no. 2 (June 1994): 129.

Watts, Tim J. *A Selected Bibliography on Workplace Privacy*. Monticello, Ill.: Vance Bibliographies, 1991.

Wetzel, Barbara A. "Asbestos in the Work Place: What Every Employee Should Know." *Santa Clara Law Review* 31, no. 2 (1991): 423.

■■■■■■■ Chapter Eight

Discipline and Discharge

*Experience is the name everyone
gives to their mistakes.*
Oscar Wilde (1854-1900)

Every manager and supervisor would like to be able to say that
all of the individuals whom they supervise are perfectly suited to
their jobs and that all perform in an exemplary manner all the time.
With any luck, most managers and supervisors are able to say that
of many, if not most of their supervisees. We approach management
of library personnel from a positive viewpoint, nonetheless knowing that we must be prepared to deal with difficult situations and
with difficult people at times.

"You had better do a good job hiring and make darn sure they
perform well during the probationary period, because once they're
past that, you can't fire them." How often have you heard managers
and supervisors lament that it has become impossible to fire anyone? Or that if you're going to discipline anyone, you'd better have
your lawyer present? No, it hasn't gotten to that point yet. But a
manager or supervisor would be wise to observe employees closely
during the probationary period and to be aware of what can and
cannot be done in the way of discipline and discharge. It may seem
as if a supervisor's hands are tied. But even though there are many
things an employer cannot do, he or she can, in a proper, legal way,
carry out discipline and discharge.

Wrongful Discipline and Discharge

In theory, an at-will employee, one who does not have a contract, may be fired for any reason. In practice, statutes and court decisions have limited somewhat the number and type of reasons for which the employer may terminate an employee. The employer may not fire an employee or otherwise discriminate against an employee in the following situations:

- In violation of the terms of a contract;

- When the employee is protected by a specific state or federal law (civil rights laws that prohibit discrimination on the basis of age, race, sex, religion, ethnicity, or disability; the First Amendment to the U.S. Constitution, which guarantees freedom of speech, freedom of religion, freedom of the press, and freedom of assembly; laws that protect the employees' rights to union activity; wage and hour laws; safety and health laws; equal pay laws; laws that prohibit discipline or discharge because an employee's wages have been attached; or workers compensation laws);

- When the employee is protected by public policy (includes protections for the employee who is forced to miss work because of jury duty or military leave);

- When the employee is protected by whistle-blower laws (laws designed to protect employees when reporting the employer for breaking the law or violating safety and health standards);

- When the employee is covered by an implied contract (a contract made orally or in an employee handbook or manual);

- When the history of the employee-employer relationship creates a duty on the employer's part to treat the employee fairly (e.g., a long-term employee with a record of faithful service).

Just Cause

Despite the limitations imposed on employers by statutes and court decisions, a number of valid, legal reasons exist for disciplining or discharging an employee. Among those reasons are

- careless destruction of company property

- conviction of a crime

- dishonesty

- drinking on the job

- racially harassing coworkers

- sexually harassing coworkers
- ethnically harassing coworkers
- excessive absences
- excessive lateness
- failing to return from approved leave
- falsifying timesheets or other official records
- fighting on the job
- gambling on the job
- gross misconduct
- incompetence
- insubordination
- lying on a job application
- negligence
- poor quality of work
- poor productivity
- possession of alcohol on the job
- possession of drugs on the job
- refusal to work
- sleeping on the job
- stealing
- unreported absences
- use of drugs on the job
- violating company rules
- violating safety rules
- walking off the job
- willful destruction of company property

Although all of the reasons why an employee cannot be disciplined or discharged are based on employee protection laws, all of the reasons for initiating action against an employee are based on what an employee does or does not do. The employer must be careful not to violate the employee's rights in the case of disciplining or terminating him or her. Here's how it should be done.

Corrective Discipline

Corrective discipline, also called progressive discipline, is designed to make employees aware of misconduct or poor performance and to give them an opportunity to correct their behavior or improve their performance. The first step in corrective discipline is to give the employee a verbal warning for minor infractions or to correct poor performance. A written warning addressed to the employee is used if the infraction or deficiency is of a more serious nature or if the employee does not heed the verbal warning. An employee may be suspended without pay for serious offenses or for continued poor performance or misconduct after previous attempts to bring about improvement have been unsuccessful. Termination is not necessarily a corrective discipline step but may be the result if previous steps of corrective discipline do not result in the desired behavior.

It is not essential that the steps be followed sequentially. Each situation must be judged independently and appropriate action taken. A specific situation may require, for example, a written warning or suspension as a first step or, in some instances, immediate discharge. The following are examples of particular steps that may be called for:

Verbal warning. Substandard work performance, unexcused absences, or tardiness.

Written warning. Continued substandard work performance, unexcused absences, or tardiness.

Suspension. Continuation of the above behaviors, insubordination, drinking or intoxication, gambling, fighting, or sleeping on the job.

The warnings and suspension are intended to allow an individual to correct a situation. The last step or first and only step in some situations is termination. Discharge is appropriate for and applicable to all previously listed examples if continued after attempts to correct, and all of the actions listed in the earlier section on just cause for termination (see pages 84-85).

Before taking any corrective, disciplinary steps, supervisors and managers are advised to consult with the appropriate authorities in the library and university.

Steps to Take Before
Terminating an Employee

The first rule in any disciplinary situation is document, document, document. It is doubly true for situations in which the employee is to be discharged. The following steps should be followed in every situation except those instances where an employee should be immediately terminated:

1. Implement the appropriate corrective discipline steps.

2. Gather all of the facts, including any that the employee may add.

3. Determine whether there is a policy that calls for discharge in this situation and be prepared to cite it.

4. Determine whether or not the employee is or should be aware of the policy.

5. Determine whether or not, in similar situations, exceptions have been made to the policy.

6. Be absolutely certain that discrimination is not involved, especially if the individual is a member of a protected class.

7. Be absolutely certain that this action is not retaliation for an earlier, unrelated act.

8. Determine whether or not this termination will make the employee a "martyr," and if so, prepare to deal with that issue with employees who remain.

9. Make certain that the employee's file contains the proper documentation supporting the termination.

10. At the time of actual termination, arrange to have another manager present.

11. Make certain that the procedures used in this termination are the same as those used in previous terminations.

How to Terminate an Employee

Before terminating an employee, make certain that the previous 11 steps have been taken. There must be written documentation defining and supporting the termination. The termination of an employee for poor performance should never come as a surprise to him or her. Through proper training, coaching, and corrective discipline steps if necessary, employees should always know where they stand. For those employees who must be terminated, however, consideration must be given to the termination interview itself and to what can and must be communicated to other employees about the termination.

Let's say that, based on all of the above-mentioned information, the decision has been made to terminate an employee. The following questions must be answered before calling in the employee:

1. *Who should terminate the employee?* The employee's supervisor must be the one who gives the message; however, another manager should be present as a witness and for support.

2. *Where should the termination meeting be held?* It must be held in a confidential setting, ideally in an empty office or conference room. That way, when you are through with the meeting, you can leave. It is difficult to walk out of your own office, and it may be difficult to get the terminated employee to leave.

3. *When should the termination meeting be held?* When planning the termination meeting, review the individual's file. To lessen the impact, avoid termination on the employee's birthday or anniversary date. Consider the employee's medical and emotional state. Does the employee anticipate termination? Friday or the day before a holiday are the worst days to plan terminations of employees. The termination meeting should be held early in the week.

4. *What will the employee be told?* You and the employee may want to discuss resignation instead of termination, if that is an option. If resignation is not an option, the termination message should be clear and irrevocable. Avoid debates and rehashes of the past. Do not allow the employee to trap you into "who said what" discussions. Make it clear that the decision has been made and that the decision is final. Be empathetic but uncompromising. Know ahead of time what you plan to say and don't let the meeting become sidetracked. Make it mercifully brief.

After the termination meeting, you will also have to resolve these questions: What will persons who inquire for references be told? What will the individual's coworkers be told?

Predischarge Rights of Public Employees

One of the most important aspects of public employment is job security. Classified employees are given a "property interest" in their jobs that cannot be taken away without "due process of law" in order to put them beyond the reach of partisan political retaliation. The rights of classified employees were established by the Lloyd-LaFollette Act of 1932.[1] The act provided classified public employees the right to postdischarge appeals and established the concept of property interest for nonprobationary public employees. Under the act, the employee must receive a written copy of the charges against him or her and a reasonable period of time in which to respond in writing to the charges. The Supreme Court ruled in the 1985 case of *Cleveland Board of Education v. Loudermill* that "the tenured public employee is entitled to oral or written notice of the charges against him, an explanation of the employer's evidence, and an opportunity to present his side of the story." It noted that "where the employer perceives a significant hazard in keeping the employee on the job, it can avoid the problem by a suspension with pay."[2] These then are the predischarge rights of public employees. When a public employee is "Loudermilled," the letter of notice has been delivered.

The Effects of Termination

Although announcements of resignations, retirements, and other voluntary terminations are often followed by departmental get-togethers, well wishes, and friendly farewells, involuntary terminations are seldom occasions for celebration. In nearly every involuntary termination, both the individuals involved and the library itself are negatively affected. The greatest impact, of course, is felt by the individual who has been discharged. Studies have shown that the level of emotional stress following termination can equal the stress of being told that one is dying of an incurable disease. The individual first suffers shock and anger, followed by the certainty that a mistake has been made. After a series of mood swings, the discharged employee may experience a period of depression. Finally, self-confidence returns. The severity of these experiences differs from individual to individual, but regardless of severity, the termination has an impact on each individual.

Coworkers may experience a mixture of shock and excitement over the news, expressing such conflicting statements as "I'm glad it didn't happen to me," "It could happen to me," "I'm sorry it happened to him," "I'm glad it happened to her," and "I'm angry with the person who fired him." Employee reaction will be affected by how well the terminated employee was liked, their perceptions of the events surrounding the termination, and their opinions of the supervisor and the administration.

The supervisor of the terminated employee may experience guilt and self-pity for having to take the action, while feeling compassion for the terminated employee. Presumably the decision to discharge has been made only after the supervisor has taken every step possible to avoid the discharge. Thus although the supervisor must be able to show compassion and empathy for the terminated employee, at the same time, he or she should feel comfortable in the correctness of the decision and the procedures taken. It is important that the terminated employee receive any assistance possible in finding another position if requested.

Every termination has its own circumstances and resulting impacts. The supervisor must be able to deal with his or her own emotions as the terminator, with the emotions of the individual terminated, and with the emotions of coworkers. A termination is successful when it is done objectively, humanely, and cleanly. It is a good termination when it can honestly be said that the result was best for all involved.

Mistakes Made in Terminations

The following mistakes made in terminations may lead to charges of discrimination or unfair treatment by persons who are terminated.

1. Documentation was lacking.

2. Performance evaluations were poorly done or not done at all.

3. The employee was unaware of the policy or that termination could be the result of his or her actions.

4. The employee was given regular salary increases that he or she interpreted as merit increases. In some cases, actual merit increases may have been given.

5. The employee was treated differently than others in similar jobs.

6. The employee had not been given sufficient help to correct substandard performance.

7. The employee had not been given a definite set of performance standards.

8. The employee was given too many "second chances."

9. The wrong person was selected to handle the termination.

10. The reasons for termination were not made clear and unequivocal.

11. Possible severe emotional reactions were not anticipated.

12. Lawsuits were not anticipated.

13. The effects on remaining employees were not anticipated.

Constructive Discharge

In order to make a case that he or she was wrongfully discharged, the former employee must be able to show that he or she was, in fact, discharged. "Terminated," "fired," "let go," "dismissed," "discharged," and "given a pink slip" all mean the same thing: You've been fired. But sometimes the sequence of events isn't quite so clear-cut. Because of "constructive discharge," a court may decide an employee was fired even though the individual quit. Constructive discharge occurs when the employer does something that makes it virtually impossible for the employee to continue on the job. For example, the court may find that an employee was constructively discharged if the employer changed working conditions, which, in turn, caused the employee to quit. The change must have been recent enough to draw a cause-and-effect relationship between the change and the resignation, and the change in working conditions has to have been so demeaning or upsetting that any reasonable person in the same situation would have quit. Being able to prove that an individual was constructively discharged is important in determining whether the former employee will receive unemployment compensation.

Gross Misconduct

Gross misconduct is one of the many just causes for termination of employees. Case law has defined gross misconduct as one of the following:

1. Deliberate or negligent disregard of the employer's interest;

2. Deliberate violations of reasonable standards of conduct set by the employer; or

3. Behavior so careless or negligent as to amount to wrongful intent.

In *Paris v. Korbel & Brothers, Inc.,* the court noted that inefficiency, poor conduct or performance, ordinary negligence, and errors in judgment are not enough for termination on the grounds of gross misconduct.[3]

The discipline and discharge of employees is the most difficult and emotionally draining part of supervision and management. Above all, the individuals who must perform these actions must understand and follow established procedures. No one wants to violate an employee's rights, but neither does one want to have a needed disciplinary action voided by an improper action. Nor is it in the best interest of the library to take no action at all for fear of making a mistake.

Right to an Appeal and
Grievance Process

This chapter thus far has dealt with the options available to employers in terms of discipline and discharge. Often, an employee believes that the employer or a fellow employee has done something that violates his or her rights. Universities, and in turn their libraries, grant to all employees the right to a grievance and appeal process. Some universities grant the same rights to student employees and permanent staff while other universities provide slightly different processes to the two groups. The difference is commonly in how far a grievance may be taken. Temporary employees and employees during their probationary period are often given access to only the first step of the process. Student employees may be considered as temporary employees in some libraries.

The primary purpose of an appeal and grievance procedure is to provide a means by which employees, without jeopardizing their jobs, can express complaints about their work or working conditions and obtain a fair hearing through progressively higher levels of management. Complaints charging discrimination based on race, creed, sex, age, sexual preference, national origin, or disability may be handled by the regular grievance procedure or be dealt with by the university's affirmative action office. The appeal and grievance procedure serves to avoid the high costs of court action, both in terms of dollars and morale.

The Two-Step Grievance Procedure

A two-step grievance and appeal process is common in university libraries. The time limits for the process may vary. In step 1, a grievance must be filed in writing by the employee within five working days following the act or discovery of the condition that gave rise to the grievance. Normally, the written grievance is submitted to an office in the personnel department of the university. A personnel officer will conduct a preliminary investigation of the grievance and attempt to mediate the dispute. If the grievance is resolved to the satisfaction of both parties, the officer prepares a report of the resolution, provides copies to both sides, and the grievance is considered closed. If the grievance is not resolved through mediation, a report to that effect is prepared and provided to both parties. If employees are given access to the second step, an appeal to step 2 of the procedure may be made.

In step 2, an appeal must be filed in writing by the employee within five working days from receipt of the step 1 report. Failure to file within the specified period constitutes forfeiture of the right to appeal, and the grievance will be considered closed. The appeal is heard by a grievance review committee, which is composed of the director of personnel, the dean or director of the library, and one other uninvolved employee selected by the aggrieved employee. The written decision of the grievance review committee, including a discussion of the case and the rationale for the decision, is provided to the employee and employer, usually within 15 working days of the hearing. There is no further right to appeal in the procedure. Any further action by the employee must be taken in civil court.

Mediation and Arbitration

In the previous two-step grievance procedure, both mediation and arbitration are used. Mediation is provided by the personnel office and arbitration by the review committee. Mediation is a procedure by which an impartial third party helps the employee and the employer to reach a voluntary agreement on how to settle a grievance. The mediator often makes suggestions or recommendations and attempts to reduce the emotions and tensions that prevent resolution of the complaint. In order to be successful, the mediator must have the trust and respect of both parties. If, in step 1, the mediator is unable to get the parties to agree, the mediation effort ends without resolution. If an appeal is made, arbitration is required. Arbitration is a procedure in which a neutral third party, in this case, the grievance review committee, studies the grievance, listens to the arguments on both sides, and makes recommendations that are binding on both sides.

Common Types of Grievances

The grievance is a formal charge made by an employee that the employee has been adversely affected by a violation of university or library policy. Grievances always allege that there has been a violation. Often the situation begins as a gripe by the employee, and when it is not handled by the supervisor to the employee's satisfaction, a grievance is filed. Some of the most common types of grievances deal with the following situations:

1. Discipline or termination for absenteeism, insubordination, misconduct, or substandard work.

2. Promotion or transfer of employees.

3. Complaints charging discrimination based on race, creed, sex, age, sexual preference, national origin, or disability.

When a Grievance Is Filed Against You

Although library management hopes that employees will never feel compelled to file grievances, they recognize that few libraries are able to completely avoid them. That is not to say that libraries with no grievances filed against them have employees who are all pleased with their jobs and their supervisors. It may be, instead, that employees are unwilling and/or afraid to bring up complaints. It is better to have problems openly discussed than to have staff who do not express their feelings. It is hoped that complaints and employee concerns can be addressed by supervisors and that grievances will not have to result. When there are many grievances filed, management must look at its supervisors.

Supervisors must know how to handle a complaint before it becomes a grievance. If a grievance is filed, it is important that the supervisor not consider it an attack on supervisor authority, only that a situation has not been resolved to the employee's satisfaction. Remember that it is the employee's right to file a grievance without jeopardizing his or her job.

If you can determine the nature of the grievance, you have taken the first step to handling it successfully. Determine if the stated complaint is the problem or if it is only a symptom of the real problem. Investigate the grievance objectively and thoroughly. One of the biggest mistakes supervisors make is to make light of complaints. The fact that an employee files a grievance indicates that the problem is important and that the employee will not be satisfied until the grievance is resolved. The supervisor must be willing to work with the mediator in a grievance; if you've made a mistake, admit it. When the grievance is resolved one way or the other, do not punish the grievant. The employee is simply exercising a right given by the university.

Alternative Dispute Resolution

Mediation and *arbitration* are terms associated with union negotiations. They have very formal meanings in the union environment—meanings that are similar to and have influenced recent use of mediation and arbitration in problem resolution in a variety of other environments as well.

A relatively new approach to the resolution of workplace problems has developed outside of the union environment: alternative dispute resolution (ADR). Mediation and arbitration are often lumped together under the heading of ADR, but there are significant differences. In mediation, two or more people or groups get a third party they trust to help them communicate with one another. The mediator doesn't represent either side but assists both sides. The mediator does not impose a decision but instead helps the parties to develop their own resolutions to the dispute. *Mediation* is usually used interchangeably with *conciliation* to mean an attempt by a third party to bring together the parties to a dispute. The mediator has no power to force a settlement but sometimes suggests compromise solutions. It is by nature a voluntary process. Where there is an aura of distrust between the disputants, each side may be unwilling to make compromises, lest these become the basis upon which bargaining takes place if the mediator's efforts ultimately fail.

Arbitration involves a situation where both sides to a dispute agree on the issues but cannot reach a resolution to the problem themselves. They agree to pick an arbitrator who will come up with a solution. Mediation and arbitration can be used when the two parties are able to agree on the issues. Neither mediation nor arbitration will work if neither party involved has any interest in continuing the relationship or wants to find a mutually agreeable way to work together.

Mediation is a highly informal process; thus much of the information about it is anecdotal. Mediation is prized for its flexibility, although it also has some drawbacks. There is no finality to it, although most mediations involve agreements on action to be taken by both parties to bring closure.

One should approach the management and supervision of library personnel from a positive viewpoint, knowing that it is important to be informed on how to handle difficult employees and how to help them succeed if possible.

References

1. The processes specified in the Lloyd-LaFollette Act were incorporated into the 1978 Civil Services Reform Act.

2. *Cleveland Board of Education v. Loudermill,* 105 S. Ct. 1487 (1985), 1495.

3. *Paris v. Korbel & Brothers, Inc.,* U.S. District Court, Northern California, No. C-89-1278 TEH (March 14, 1990).

Bibliography

Bies, Robert, Christopher Martin, and Joel Brockner. "Just Laid Off, But Still a 'Good Citizen?' Only If the Process Is Fair." *Employee Responsibilities and Rights Journal* 6, no. 3 (September 1993): 227.

Dilts, David A., and Clarence R. Deitsch. "The Tests of Just Cause: What Price Predictability in Arbitral Decision Making." *Employee Responsibilities and Rights Journal* 5, no. 1 (March 1992): 13.

Dworkin, Terry Morehead, and Melissa S. Baucus. "Wrongful Firing in Violation of Public Policy: Who Gets Fired and Why." *Employee Responsibilities and Rights Journal* 7, no. 3 (September 1994): 191.

Fox, Jeremy B., and Hugh D. Hindman. "The Model Employment Termination Act: Provisions and Discussion." *Employee Responsibilities and Rights Journal* 6, no. 1 (March 1993): 33.

Jacobs, Carol S. "The Use of the Exit Interview as a Personnel Tool and Its Applicability to Libraries." *Journal of Library Administration* 14, no. 4 (1991): 69.

Johnson, Kathryn A. "Constructive Discharge and 'Reasonable Accommodation' Under the Americans with Disabilities Act." *University of Colorado Law Review* 65, no. 1 (1993): 175.

Kaplan, Andrew B. "How to Avoid Wrongful Discharge Lawsuits." *Journal of Accountancy* 169, no. 5 (May 1990): 87.

Kaplan, Andrew B. "How to Fire Without Fear." *The Personnel Administrator* 34, no. 3 (September 1989): 74.

Kelley, Mark W. "Constructive Discharge: A Suggested Standard for West Virginia and Other Jurisdictions." *West Virginia Law Review* 93, no. 4 (summer 1991): 1047.

Klaas, Brian, and Hoyt Wheeler. "Supervisors and Their Response to Poor Performance: A Study of Disciplinary Decision Making." *Employee Responsibilities and Rights Journal* 5, no. 4 (December 1992): 339.

Kriegler, Roy. "Dismissal: Employee Rights and Procedural Fairness." *Law Institute Journal* 65, no. 12 (December 1991): 1158.

Morin, William J., and Lyle Yorks. *Dismissal: There Is No Easy Way But There Is a Better Way.* New York: Drake Beam Morin, 1990.

Petersen, Donald J. "The Arbitration of Fighting Cases." *The International Journal of Conflict Management* 2, no. 3 (July 1991): 201.

Petersen, Donald J. "Quits, Recision of Quits and Constructive Discharge in Arbitration." *Employee Responsibilities and Rights Journal* 3, no. 2 (June 1990): 125.

"Promoting Fairness: A Proposal for a More Reasonable Standard of Constructive Discharge in Title VII Denial of Promotion Cases." *The Fordham Urban Law Journal* 19, no. 4 (summer 1992): 979.

Shepard, Ira Michael. *Workplace Privacy: Employee Testing, Surveillance, Wrongful Discharge, and Other Areas of Vulnerability*, 2nd ed. Washington, D.C.: Bureau of National Affairs, 1989.

Thornton, Gene R. "Labor and Employment Review: Rights of Terminated Employees: Expanding Remedies." *Colorado Lawyer* 21, no. 8 (August 1992): 1639.

"Who Says Quitters Never Win?" *Small Business Report* 19, no. 10 (October 1994): 45.

"Wrongful Discharge: Recovery for Emotional Distress Damages Caused by Discharge Based on Workers Compensation Claim." *Law Reporter* 34, no. 2 (March 1991): 74.

Youngblood, Stuart, Linda Trevino, and Monica Favia. "Reactions to Unjust Dismissal and Third-Party Dispute Resolution: A Justice Framework." *Employee Responsibilities and Rights Journal* 5, no. 4 (December 1992): 283.

■■■■■■■ Chapter Nine

Income Replacement

*While times are quiet, it is easy to
take action; ere coming troubles have
cast their shadows, it is easy to lay plans.*
Lao Tzu (6th century B.C.)

There are essentially three programs that provide income to individuals whose employment is interrupted. For individuals who cannot work because of work-related injury or illness, there is workers compensation. For individuals who cannot work for at least 12 months because of injury or illness, there is social security disability insurance. For individuals who have lost their job through no fault of their own, there is unemployment insurance. These three programs are the focus of this chapter.

Workers Compensation

Prior to the establishment of workers compensation laws, if an employee was injured at work, he or she was simply replaced. The injured employee was forced to file a private lawsuit against the employer to recover medical costs and lost wages. The employers in these lawsuits were able to use one of three defenses: contributory negligence, assumption of the risk, or the fellow servant rule.

Contributory negligence was used as a defense by employers to show that the individual was negligent and, consequently, caused the injury. If the injured employee had been doing the job correctly, there would not have been an accident. A second defense, *assumption of the risk*, implied that the employee knew that the job was a dangerous one and, by agreeing to do the job, assumed the risk. Under a third defense, the *fellow-servant rule*, the employer could claim that a coworker was the cause of an accident and that the injured employee must sue the coworker.

Lawsuits against coworkers and employers resulted in hardships for the employees and in some cases, where the employer was found to be at fault, bankruptcies. Liability lawsuits for on-the-job injuries led to the development of workers compensation laws.

Quite simply, workers compensation laws provide that the employee who is injured in a job-related accident cannot sue the employer but will be provided with medical care and continued income while unable to work. Workers compensation laws require that the employer carry insurance that will pay all of the injured employee's medical expenses and protect the employee against loss of income if the employee is hurt in an on-the-job accident or contracts an illness related to the job. Workers compensation laws are also intended to protect the employee against discipline by the employer for filing workers compensation claims. It is essentially a no-fault system that makes no distinction about who is at fault for the accident.

Workers compensation laws were enacted and are administered by individual states. Although some of the requirements vary from state to state, the laws and court decisions governing workers compensation follow a pattern. Generally speaking, the workers compensation laws in all 50 states assume the following sequence of events:

- The employer purchases workers compensation insurance or, in some instances, is self-insured.

- The employee is injured on the job or contracts an illness that is related to the job.

- The insurance carrier begins immediate payment for medical, hospital, and surgical bills.

- The employee files a claim for workers compensation and the employer's insurance carrier begins paying the employee benefits based on a percentage of the employee's average weekly income (66 2/3 percent of gross up to a maximum cap in most states).

- The employee is not required to pay income taxes on workers compensation benefits.

- The state workers compensation board approves the employee's claim if they find it to be work-related.

- The insurance carrier continues to pay the employee's medical bills and income benefits for the duration of the employee's disability.

- As the employee's condition improves, he or she returns to "light duty."

- Eventually the employee is back to full duty and off workers compensation, or the employee cannot return to full duty and workers compensation makes up the difference between what the employee was able to earn before the accident and what he or she can earn with the disability.

- If the employee is disabled, the employer must make accommodations in accordance with the Americans with Disabilities Act (ADA).

For most injuries and occupational diseases, workers compensation laws usually provide:

1. immediate medical benefits;

2. prompt periodic wage replacement for a specified number of weeks;

3. if applicable, a death benefit;

4. if applicable, payment for loss of function or disfigurement; and

5. vocational retraining services if the employee is unable to return to the former job.

In addition, employers in many states are required to:

1. continue the injured worker's group health and life insurance;

2. provide suitable work, if available, when the injured worker is able to return to "light duty";

3. return the recovered worker to the former job or an equivalent job if one is available; and

4. refrain from any form of retaliation against the worker for filing a workers compensation claim.

Administration of Workers Compensation

The workers compensation laws are administered and enforced by each state's workers compensation commission or board. This agency establishes rules and regulations regarding how and when claims for benefits must be made, how and when claims may be contested, and how and when hearings and appeals are scheduled. Most states require employers to have workers compensation coverage for their employees, although a few make it elective.

Most employees in most states are covered by workers compensation with the following exceptions: longshoremen and harbor workers, railroad workers, and federal employees. Maritime workers are covered by the Longshoremen's and Harbor Workers Compensation Act (LHWCA); railroad workers are covered by the Federal Employers' Liability Act (FELA); and federal workers are covered by the Federal Employees' Compensation Act (FECA).

Another group of persons not covered by workers compensation laws are independent contractors. Independent contractors are not covered because they are technically not employees of the institution. Most institutions have procedures by which independent contractors are identified. One procedure is to use the IRS test of "common law factors" to make the determination. If the employee can answer "no" to the following questions, that employee is eligible to be an independent contractor:

- Do I get training or instruction on how to do the job?

- Do I perform the task in person, on company property, and during set hours?

- Is there a continuing work relationship?

- Do I work exclusively for one institution?

- Am I paid by the hour, week, or month, rather than by the job?

- Am I reimbursed for business and travel expenses?

- Does the institution provide my tools or equipment?

- Can I be fired or can I quit without any contractual liability?

If the employee is an independent contractor, that employee is not eligible for workers compensation coverage.

Eligibility for Benefits

An employee is eligible for workers compensation benefits when an injury or illness "arises out of and in the course of employment." For an employee to be eligible, that person must have been injured:

during work time;

in a place where the employee was supposed to be or at least could have reasonably been expected to have been;

in the line of duty; and,

under circumstances where there is a cause-and-effect relationship between the job and the injury.

Situations Where Workers Compensation Is Requested

The following are some of the most common situations where workers compensation benefits are requested:

Commuting. Injuries incurred when en route to or from work are not generally covered by workers compensation. Hazards faced by employees on their way to and from work are common to the public at large and are not specifically work-related.

Special hazards. It is the special hazards presented by the job that workers compensation is designed to cover, such as when an employee is injured in a location because the job required that he or she be in a specific location.

Dual purpose trips. Employees are covered if injured on a business trip even if that trip involved both business and pleasure. The controlling factor, business or pleasure, determines whether the employee is covered by workers compensation. If the reason an individual is at a specific place is business, that employee's injury is covered by workers compensation.

On call. If an employee is injured when called to work while on call for emergencies, the employee's injury would be covered by workers compensation. Generally, simply being called to work early or late does not qualify as on call because it lacks urgency.

Parking lots. Generally, injuries that occur in the employer's parking lot are covered by workers compensation if the employer owns the parking lot.

Making deliveries. If injured while making deliveries or while being driven from one job site to another in a company vehicle, employees are covered. If injured while deviating from the usual route, the determination of coverage is based on the extent of the deviation and its purpose.

Asleep on the job. Workers accidentally injured while asleep on the job have generally been ruled eligible for benefits.

Athletic teams. The degree to which the employer is involved determines whether or not an employee who is injured while playing for a company team is covered by workers compensation.

Office parties and picnics. Employees are covered by workers compensation during office parties and picnics if the employer pays for the party or picnic and employees are expected to attend, if the party or picnic is held on work premises, or if the party or picnic is held during work time.

Situations Where Workers Compensation May Be Denied

The following are some of the situations under which workers compensation benefits do not apply:

Violation of rules. If injured while fooling around in violation of company rules, an employee may be excluded from coverage.

Willful misconduct. An injury may not be covered if it is caused by an employee's own willful and serious misconduct. It would be covered if the cause was a fellow employee's misconduct.

Alcohol and drugs. An injury caused by an employee's intoxication or addiction to alcohol or drugs is not normally covered by workers compensation.

Fighting. Injuries caused by fights between employees may not be covered; however, an injury incurred while protecting the employer's property or interests or if connected to some job duty may be covered.

Occupational Illness or Disease

Occupational illness or disease is different from accidental injury in that the proof required to obtain workers compensation is different. In addition, although accidental injury is unexpected, occupational illnesses really aren't. Thus occupational illnesses relate to their "reasonableness" of occurring. For example, carpal tunnel syndrome, or repetitive motion disorder, is a reasonably common problem among workers who use computers extensively in their work. It is found to be an occupational illness for the purposes of workers compensation if it results from continued exposure to a recognized hazard of a particular job. In this instance, an individual who is required to work at a keyboard for long hours might reasonably develop carpal tunnel syndrome and have a workers compensation claim, while an individual whose daily routine involves very little keyboard work may not.

Filing a Workers Compensation Claim

Because every state has its own workers compensation laws, the procedures for filing workers compensation claims differ. However, they are similar in their basic requirements. Most states require that the employee notify the employer within a specified period that a claim is being filed. In order to be eligible for disability benefits, the employer must be notified in a timely fashion. Proper notice should include the employee's name, address, occupation, and the employer's name and address, the date and site of the accident that caused the injury or the date the employee first noticed symptoms of the occupational disease, and a description of the injury or disease. The claim for workers compensation benefits should clearly state the connection between the injury or disease and the job. State laws also require that a claim be filed with the state's workers compensation agency.

The employer has the right to contest an employee's workers compensation claim, usually within a specific period of time. The employer has the right to require the employee to submit to a medical examination to determine the extent of the employee's injury or the degree of rehabilitation.

Hearing and Appeals Process

In the case of a contested claim, there is a hearing process and avenues of appeal for workers compensation claims. A typical process is as follows:

Informal hearing. First, a workers compensation commissioner convenes an informal hearing at which the employee and employer state their cases. The commissioner will attempt to mediate an agreement.

Formal hearing. If not resolved at the informal hearing, the workers compensation commissioner will schedule a formal hearing at which the employee and employer may be represented by attorneys. The commissioner may call witnesses and hear testimony. Although it is a formal hearing, the commissioner is not required to follow rules of evidence or legal procedure. After the hearing, the commissioner normally has up to a couple of months to render a decision.

Appeals. Either party may appeal the commissioner's ruling to the workers compensation review board. Further appeal may be made to the appellate court, which will hear only questions of law and not questions of fact.

Civil Lawsuits

Workers compensation laws were established to provide employees with income replacement for work-related injuries or illnesses, and to protect employers from costly lawsuits. If employees are injured or contract an illness that is attributable to the job, they cannot sue the employer but must avail themselves of the workers compensation laws. However, if an injury or illness is found not to fall within the purview of workers compensation, the employee may file a civil lawsuit. Instances where workers compensation laws do not apply include (1) injuries caused by a third party, (2) intentional injuries, (3) motor vehicle cases, and (4) ADA violations.

If an employee's injury is caused by the negligence of a third party who is neither an employer or coworker, the employee may sue that individual. For example, an employee who is injured while making a delivery in a company vehicle can sue the driver of the car that runs a red light.

Employees may bring civil lawsuits against the employer or a coworker for intentional injuries. For example, an employee who is injured in a fight with a coworker may bring a private lawsuit for assault and battery. Some states also allow an employee to sue fellow employees for injuries caused by the negligent operation of a motor vehicle.

Finally, discrimination charges may be made under the ADA, if, for example, the employee is a qualified disabled individual as a result of a job-related injury.

Social Security Disability Insurance

When the employee and employer pay into the social security program, they are automatically purchasing long-term disability insurance coverage. Employees who pay into the program for a specified period of time become eligible for benefits in the event that they become unable to earn a living. In all but the most unusual cases, the social security system is not concerned with how an individual became disabled, only that the disability prevents that individual from performing any job or that the disability is expected to keep the individual out of work for a year or more. For example, an individual suffers severe injuries in an automobile accident and is unable to work for at least a year. That individual would qualify for coverage under social security disability insurance.

Filing a Social Security Disability Insurance Claim

Individuals filing for social security disability benefits must file immediately because there is a five-month waiting period before the individual can begin receiving payments. If a social security disability claim is approved, the monthly checks for the individual will be roughly equivalent to those received by a retired person with a similar wage or salary history in the years just before retirement. Extra benefits may be awarded for dependents. The local Social Security Administration office has the forms and formulas required to determine the benefit amounts for individuals.

Because not all individuals who are injured and unable to work remain disabled for life, the social security disability insurance program includes various efforts to help individuals rehabilitate so they can go back to work. At various times, agencies concerned with rehabilitation contact the individual to determine the status of the disability. If the individual's condition shows promise for rehabilitation, these agencies will provide the support and training needed to get the individual back into the workplace. During the attempt to return to work the social security disability insurance program continues to make disability payments. Individuals may return to work for up to nine months without losing benefits to see whether they can work. If the trial is successful, the individual continues to receive social security checks for two more months to assist with the transition back to work.

Hearing and Appeals Process

If an individual's claim for social security disability benefits is denied, there are four levels of appeals available.

1. *Request for reconsideration.* The individual may review the Social Security Administration's files and submit corrections or additional information that may cause the agency to reverse its decision.

2. *Administrative hearing.* The individual may request a hearing by an independent administrative law judge who may (1) issue a ruling based on the evidence already submitted; (2) issue a ruling based on additional written information submitted; or (3) issue a ruling based on a hearing held to present new or more detailed information.

3. *Review by appeals council.* The individual may request a review by the Social Security Appeals Council in Washington, D.C. The council can decide whether or not to hear an appeal. If it decides to hear an appeal, the individual may submit a written argument or appear in person.

4. *Federal court.* If the individual fails to get approval at any of the previous levels, a private lawsuit may be filed in federal court to order the Social Security Administration to honor the individual's claim.

Unemployment Insurance

One of the least understood of the income replacement programs is unemployment insurance. Simply stated, the unemployment insurance system is a sort of government-imposed severance pay policy. It was designed to provide partial income to individuals to tide them over during short periods of unemployment. Employers pay quarterly taxes to finance both state and federal unemployment insurance systems. Founded in 1935, the unemployment insurance system is run jointly by the federal government and the 50 states. State systems provide benefits to qualified unemployed persons for a limited period of time, normally 26 weeks. The federal unemployment insurance system is designed to finance extended benefits in times of high unemployment. For example, unemployment benefits are extended by an additional 13 weeks for all employees whose original benefit period ran out after March 1, 1991.

Unemployment insurance covers all employees, including part-time and temporary employees. To be covered the employee must have worked for a substantial period and earned a minimum amount. In most states, the individual must have been employed for at least six months during the year before the job loss. Employees need not be U.S. citizens but must be eligible to work in the United States. Persons not covered by the unemployment insurance system include individuals working for the college or university they attend, individuals employed by small farms, casual domestic workers and baby-sitters, minor newspaper carriers, children employed by their parents, employees of religious organizations, and elected officials.

Eligibility for Unemployment Insurance Benefits

An individual must meet two basic requirements to be eligible for unemployment insurance benefits: (1) the employee must be available to be recalled to his or her old job or to work in a similar one; and (2) the employee must be physically able to perform the old job or a similar one.

The reasons an individual may be disqualified from receiving benefits vary from state to state, but the most common reasons are as follows:

- The employee was fired from the job for misconduct.

- The employee was fired for just cause.

- The employee was fired for committing a felony in the course of employment.

- The employee refused to accept a similar job without good reason.

- The employee went out on strike.

- The employee is serving a prison sentence.

- The employee voluntarily retired.

- The employee quit the job without a good reason.

Disputes over unemployment insurance claims often come because of disagreements over why an employee quit. The following "good reasons" are usually considered good enough to qualify an individual for unemployment insurance benefits:

- Some form of fraud was involved in recruiting an individual for the job; for example, the employee was promised one salary and given a lower salary.

- The employee's life or health was being endangered by the employer's failure to maintain a healthy and safe workplace.

- The employee's job was dramatically changed from what that person was hired to perform.

- The employee's wages and benefits were substantially reduced.

- The employee was being sexually harassed on the job and the employer failed to take action.

- The employee was constructively discharged.

- A change in the location of the work made it impractical for the employee to continue.

Once eligible for unemployment insurance benefits, the individual must remain eligible by actively seeking employment and accepting a suitable job when one is offered.

Filing an Unemployment Insurance Claim

Claims for unemployment insurance benefits are accepted and paid by the states through thousands of offices throughout the United States. Once the claim is filed, the state's unemployment office will verify the claim by sending an inquiry to the former employer, who must respond, either verifying or disputing the circumstances surrounding the individual's claim.

Generally, an agency representative will make an initial determination of eligibility, which either party may dispute. Appeals are generally held before a referee. The referee may confirm, change, or reverse the initial award or denial of benefits. Appeal of that decision is to an agency review panel, which will review the written documentation. Further appeals can be made to the civil courts.

The unemployment insurance system is set up to provide benefits to unemployed workers and begins with the assumption that when the individual loses his or her job, that person is entitled to receive benefits. Once the former employee files a claim and it is approved, it is up to the employer to contest the claim for benefits and prove that the individual is ineligible. For many employers, appealing the decision is not worth the trouble even though high turnover means higher unemployment insurance rates. In some states, as many as 90 percent of the claimants who are discharged by their employers are awarded benefits, and fully one third of those who voluntarily quit are successful in getting unemployment benefits. Even when employers do appeal, they often lose because they do not have work rules, or if they have work rules, they fail to apply them consistently, and they fail to document previous disciplinary steps.[1]

Other Income Replacement Options

Although workers compensation, social security disability insurance, and unemployment compensation provide the most substantial amounts of replacement income when an employee is out of work, there are other options for individuals, including:

• private disability insurance

• state disability programs

• withdrawals from pension plans (some pension programs allow withdrawals prior to retirement for emergency purposes)

• food stamps

- veteran benefits (available to veterans who become unable to work because of a disability)

- supplemental social security (a program that provides money to low-income disabled persons)

- medicare (provides assistance to disabled persons when an injury or illness prevents that person from working)

- disaster benefits (for individuals who have lost their jobs because of disaster)

Reference

1. Lewin G. Joel III, *Every Employee's Guide to the Law: Everything You Need to Know About Your Rights in the Workplace—And What to Do If They Are Violated* (New York: Pantheon, 1993), 282.

Bibliography

Bahls, C. Steven. "Application of Workers' and Unemployment Compensation Statutes to Limited Liability Companies." *Montana Law Review* 55, no. 2 (summer 1994): 387.

Baig, Ellen Fell. "Workers Compensation Law." *Nova Law Review* 18, no. 1 (fall 1993): 427.

Baker, David, and Gregory Sones. "Employer Obligations to Reinstate Injured Workers—Relating Human Rights Legislation to S. 54b of the Workers' Compensation Act." *Journal of Law and Social Policy* 5/6 (1989): 30.

Barth, Peter S. "Worker's Compensation for Mental Stress Cases." *Behavioral Sciences & the Law* 8, no. 4 (fall 1990): 349.

Bober, Gerald Marvin, and Michael Wible. "Compensable Injury or Death Arising Under the Longshore and Harbor Workers' Compensation Act." *Loyola Law Review* 35, no. 4 (winter 1990): 1129.

Burr, Timothy F., and Scott A. Soule. "Longshore and Harbor Workers' Compensation Act." *Loyola Law Review* 38, no. 3 (fall 1992): 620.

Camilleri, Michael, Lynn Szymoniak, and Lori Lovgren. "Workers Compensation Law: Recent Developments." *Tort & Insurance Law Journal* 29, no. 2 (winter 1994): 452.

"The Compensability of Post-Traumatic Stress Disorder Under Oklahoma Workers Compensation Laws." *Tulsa Law Journal* 25, no. 4 (summer 1990): 815.

"Employee Rape Cases: Are Workers Compensation Benefits an Employee's Exclusive Remedy?" *Cumberland Law Review* 20, no. 3 (1989): 801.

Furman, James, and Helene Leichter. "What the New Workers Compensation Law Means to Public Employers." *Western City* 69, no. 9 (September 1993): 18.

Hersh, Adam. "Go Home Stranger: An Analysis of Unequal Workers Compensation Death Benefits to Nonresident Alien Beneficiaries." *Florida State University Law Review* 22, no. 1 (summer 1994): 217.

Ison, Terence G. "Rights to Employment Under the Workers Compensation Acts and Other Statutes." *Osgoode Hall Law Journal* 28, no. 4 (winter 1990): 839.

Matthews, Joseph L. *Social Security, Medicare and Pensions*, 4th ed. Berkeley, Calif.: Nolo Press, 1988.

McDole, Gregory J. "Strategies for Cost Control in Workers Compensation Claims: Cities Fight Back." *Preventive Law Reporter* 12, no. 2 (summer 1993): 6.

McElveen, Junius C., Jr. "Recent Trends in Workers Compensation." *Employee Relations Law Journal* 18, no. 2 (fall 1992): 245.

Murphy, James P. "Proving a Defense of Fraudulent Employment Application in Workers Compensation Accident Claims." *Bridgeport Law Review* 13, no. 4 (winter 1993): 857.

Neumann, Lee Anne. "Workers Compensation and High Stress Occupations: Application of Wisconsin's Unusual Stress Test to Law Enforcement Post-Traumatic Stress Disorder." *Marquette Law Review* 77, no. 1 (fall 1993): 147.

Nordstrom, Rodney R. "Suicide as a Compensable Injury Under Workers Compensation Statutes: A Review of Judicial Decisions." *Employee Relations Law Journal* 16, no. 1 (summer 1990): 37.

O'Kasey, Karen. "Recent Developments in Workers Compensation Law." *Tort & Insurance Law Journal* 30, no. 2 (winter 1995): 627.

Quinones, M. Carlos. "Workers Compensation Law—The Sexual Harassment Claim Quandary: Workers Compensation as an Inadequate and Unavailable Remedy: Cox v. Chino Mines/Phelps Dodge." *New Mexico Law Review* 24, no. 3 (summer 1994): 565.

Richman, Stephen I. "Reasoned Decisions in Workers Compensation Cases." *Workers Compensation Law Review* 15 (1992): 441.

Schwartz, Gary T. "Waste, Fraud, and Abuse in Workers Compensation: The Recent California Experience." *Maryland Law Review* 52, no. 4 (1993): 983.

Somner, Christine L. "Worker's Compensation and Company Sponsored Events: The High Cost of Employee Morale." *Cleveland State Law Review* 39, no. 2 (1991): 181.

Spieler, Emily A. "Perpetuating Risk? Workers Compensation and the Persistence of Occupational Injuries." *Houston Law Review* 31, no. 1 (1994): 119.

Stern, Carole, and Cathleen M. Tierney. "Inheriting Workplace Risks: The Effect of Workers Compensation 'Exclusive Remedy' Clauses on the Preconception Tort After Johnson Controls." *Tort & Insurance Law Journal* 28, no. 4 (summer 1993): 800.

Vance, Ruth C. "Workers Compensation and Sexual Harassment in the Workplace: A Remedy for Employees, or a Shield for Employers?" *Hofstra Labor Law Journal* 11, no. 1 (fall 1993): 141.

Wettstein, Robert M. "Introduction to Workers Compensation." *Behavioral Sciences & the Law* 8, no. 4 (fall 1990): 329.

Wilcox, R. Vickie. "Workers Compensation Law—Pursuing the 'Benevolent Purpose' of New Mexico's Workers Compensation Statute as a Reimbursement Statute: *Montoya v. AKAL Security, Inc.*" *New Mexico Law Review* 24, no. 3 (summer 1994): 577.

■■■■■■■ Chapter Ten

What to Do Before
You Phone the Attorney

*The difficult things of this world must once
have been easy; the great things of this world
must once have been small. Set about difficult
things while they are still easy; do great things
while they are still small.*

Lao Tzu (6th century B.C.)

In the day-to-day management of an academic library, supervisors, managers, and administrators encounter any number of personnel problems. These problems may be of the minor variety that seem to consume inordinate amounts of time. Yet, problems that were once small, as Lao Tzu suggests, can become large if left unattended. Such problems may ultimately challenge even the most experienced administrator and involve the university's administration and legal counsel. The problems faced by supervisors, managers, and administrators may involve librarians, staff, or student employees. Or they might involve students, faculty, or library patrons. They may involve friends, relatives, or acquaintances of the employee. They may involve violations of individual employee rights; library and/or university rules, policies, or procedures; or violations of civil or criminal laws. There appears, to the harried supervisor, to be no end to the kinds of difficulties that can occur. Personnel problems addressed here cover the gamut of personnel management, from the minor to the major, handled easily internally or involving university administration, campus police, and attorneys.

Violations of Employee Rights

As an indication of how strained the employer-employee relationship is becoming in some instances, consider the advice given by Lewin G. Joel III in the book *Every Employee's Guide to the Law: Everything You Need to Know About Your Rights in the Workplace—And What to Do If They Are Violated*. Joel suggests that individuals purchase accordion file folders before setting out to get a job. He advises that everything from the first application for a job to the employee handbook to performance evaluations and every piece of paper relating to the job be kept in the file in anticipation of filing a lawsuit against the employer. He says that because the employer keeps a file it is important for the employee to keep one too.[1]

As evidenced by the previous chapters, many laws and policies exist to protect employee and employer rights. We live in a litigious society, with everyone seemingly ready to sue at the drop of a hat. It is important in this environment that everyone understand the ground rules established by the law and that managers be prepared to deal effectively with personnel difficulties that arise, without violating anyone's rights. Those rights are spelled out in some detail in previous chapters and fall within the following categories:

- rights protected by a specific state or federal law

- civil rights laws that prohibit discrimination

- rights protected by the First Amendment to the U.S. Constitution

- employees' rights to union activity

- rights protected by wage and hour laws

- rights protected by safety and health laws

- rights protected by equal pay laws

- rights protected by laws that prohibit discipline or discharge because an employee's wages have been attached

- rights protected by workers compensation laws

- rights protected by public policy

- rights protected by whistle-blower laws

- rights covered by an implied contract

Mine Fields

Library supervisors, managers, and administrators must be cognizant of the areas in which many personnel difficulties occur. Such situations lend themselves to potential problems because (1) they involve legally protected rights, or (2) they involve the employer's taking action against an employee and the employee seeking to find a way out of the difficulty. Those most difficult situations include the job interview; the hiring process; performance evaluations; promotions; salary and merit determinations; dealing with poor performance; reassignment; discipline; demotion; suspension; termination; personal problems; and the exit interview. There are also situations in which the employee is the victim or the perpetrator of an activity that is just cause for termination and/or is illegal. Occasionally, employees are the victims of stalking, obscene phone calls, harassment, theft, drug or alcohol abuse in the family, domestic violence, or personal financial problems.

Whether the situation involves a personnel action or illegal activity, library supervisors, managers, and administrators are faced with a minefield of potential difficulty. The following scenarios are presented with the purpose of providing managers with suggested solutions. The situations, circumstances, and the people involved differ from one problem to another. The administrator, manager, or supervisor will have to evaluate each problem individually and decide what course of action would be the most appropriate for the employee and the library. This determination will often involve other individuals, most notably the library's administrators and personnel specialists and, often, the university's administration, law enforcement, and legal staff.

Many problems can be resolved by talking to or counseling employees. Care must be taken, however, not to cross the line into an area that must be reserved for those professionals who have the proper training to counsel persons with emotional problems. Inappropriate advice may do more to complicate the problem than to solve it for the employee.

Before labeling an employee the source of a problem, consider the possibility that the cause of the problem may be poor management. Research studies have found that about half of the employees labeled problems by supervisors were victims of poor supervision. These employees had not been adequately trained, had not been given counseling when needed, or had not received written warnings when required. Supervisors who do not have the patience or the ability to help employees or change their behavior should resolve to improve or seriously consider getting out of supervision.

The Job Interview

THE PROBLEM. Yolanda, Brian, and Wanda sat at the small table in the catalog department's meeting room. Brian and Wanda were senior library specialists appointed by Yolanda to assist her in hiring a new staff member. Yolanda was the librarian in charge of the department.

"I've called this meeting to review what we will be doing in the coming weeks," stated Yolanda. "As you know, the library tech position has been posted by the human resources department. The application deadline is Friday. After a few days we will be receiving the pool of applications to review. We will use the screening grid we developed earlier, which lists all of the required and desired qualifications. We will review each application and assign points to each applicant based on the posted qualifications. At that point we will make a decision on who should be interviewed based on the number of points received."

Yolanda paused for a moment, then continued. "During the interviews, we will ask each candidate the list of questions we developed earlier. Remember to bring your list of inappropriate questions just to be sure we don't stray into those areas. The only reason we will ask questions not on our list is in order to get the candidate to expand on a specific answer. Do you have any questions?"

"Yes," said Brian. "What can we tell people who ask about the hiring?"

"If people in the department, or anyone else for that matter, ask about the hiring, simply tell them that this is a confidential process," responded Yolanda. "We can't discuss the pool, any person in the pool, or even respond to questions about whether or not individuals are in the pool. When we set up interviews, people who are in the pool and are being interviewed will know, and people in the pool who are not being interviewed will know that, but our position is that we will not discuss any aspect of the hiring until someone has been offered the job, has accepted, and we have a start date. At that time, it will be announced and everyone will know. Be prepared to have people try to get information from you, but don't discuss it in any way. Change the subject if you can. This is a confidential process."

"What about Mary? Everyone knows that she wants the job. Is it going to be Mary's job?" Wanda asked.

"No, it is not Mary's job," answered Yolanda. "I know that she wants the job, but she will have to compete with everyone else who wants the job." For a moment, Yolanda looked worried. Then she continued, "Please don't, under any circumstances, talk to Mary about the job. If she turns out to be the most qualified person for the position and, based on her qualifications and the interview, is the best person, we will recommend she be hired. But if you hear people say it is Mary's job, tell them that we will recommend that the most qualified person be hired. If other applicants heard that this was Mary's job, and Mary is hired, they can sue the library and the university on the grounds that there was preselection. If you hear the rumor, please help us stop it."

Six weeks later, Mary is hired for the position, and Ted, another finalist for the position, filed a complaint that the library had known all along that it was going to hire Mary for the position, although he could cite no evidence of it. Ted also claimed that he was asked by one of the staff during his interview whether he rented or owned his home, and hadn't his neighborhood been cited by the police for gang crimes?

RESOLVING THE PROBLEM. If a claim of discrimination in the job interview is filed by an applicant, the parties named in the suit can only wait for the claim to be investigated. In the usual order of things, the university will receive notification of the claim and will participate in defending the suit. In the event of a claim, it will become important that you have thought to have a witness or witnesses present for the interview. All of the hiring documentation needs to be reviewed and made available upon request.

PREVENTING THE PROBLEM. Although department staff maintained confidentiality in the process and there was no preselection, inappropriate questions were asked in the interview. As discussed in Chapter 2, care must be taken in asking questions. Generally speaking, questions relating to the following cannot be asked before hiring: age, marital status or family, citizenship, national origin, group memberships, religion, race, sex, disabilities, arrests and convictions, military service, and height, weight, or other physical attributes. In this instance, whether the applicant owned or rented his home and the comment on his neighborhood are irrelevant and could be used to unfairly single out minorities. It is recommended that interviewers confine their questions to matters relating to job experience, education, and training, and that the applicant's references be contacted.

All library supervisors, managers, and administrators who have hiring responsibilities must be made aware of what constitutes inappropriate interview questions. Any interviewing should be done by at least two individuals. One or both of the individuals should be taking note of what is said in response to interview questions and be alert to the types of questions that are asked. Having an additional person or persons present in the interview provides a witness or witnesses to the interview in the event discrimination is claimed by an applicant.

The Hiring Process

THE PROBLEM. Andrew was both sad and happy that Sarah had gotten the position she applied for downtown. The position offered a very nice salary and at a location closer to her home. Now the highest level staff position in the reference department was vacant and the hiring process was grinding to an end. Monica had come to him earlier and expressed her interest in Sarah's former position. Monica was well qualified and had been a solid performer in the department for a number of years. Andrew had told her how to apply and even notified her when the posting was available. He had worked closely with two of the most senior staff in the department in screening the applications and conducting the interviews.

Monica was one of three individuals interviewed by the three of them. It had been a clear-cut decision agreed to by all three members of the hiring committee. A person employed by a nearby library had been offered the position. Monica was furious. Andrew recalled his last conversation with Monica. She had listened calmly to his explanation of why she hadn't been offered the job. When he had finished, she simply said, "But, Andrew, you promised me the job. You lied to me." Now, Andrew was looking at the EEOC claim of discrimination. Monica, who was 48 years old, was claiming age discrimination.

RESOLVING THE PROBLEM. Once the interviews are completed and the references for the finalists have been contacted, a job offer is made. It is not unusual for individuals in the pool, whether they were semifinalists or not, to inquire about who was hired and why they were not hired. Typically, the office handling the hiring process, often the university's human resources office, retains all of the paperwork for the hiring. That office normally has a procedure by which individuals not selected for the position may request information on who was hired and information relating to why they were not hired. It is important that the hiring supervisor conscientiously record the reasons for not hiring, reasons that are related directly to the individual's qualifications for the job. Poor documentation of the reasons for not hiring is the primary cause of claims of discrimination in the hiring process. Assembling the paperwork required to document the hiring can be done in consultation with the other individual(s) involved in the interview process. Proper training and procedures are very important in developing and completing hiring packets.

PREVENTING THE PROBLEM. Complaints are often lodged by individuals already employed by the library who are applying for promotion to vacant positions. It is common for other individuals to be selected for those positions for very good reasons, leaving the library employee to inquire as to why he or she was not selected. A common error made by hiring supervisors is to let the individual who is already on board believe that he or she will be hired into the promotional position and encourage the feeling that the hiring process will most surely lead to his or her promotion. When a more qualified candidate is found and must be hired, the sense of betrayal is common. Care must be taken not to promise anything except that everyone's application will be carefully considered. Preselection must be avoided at all costs. Make certain that internal candidates for vacancies understand that the most qualified candidate will be hired.

Dealing with Discrimination Problems

In a nondiscriminatory library, supervisors, managers, and administrators are committed to hiring, promoting, and otherwise dealing with all persons based solely on their individual abilities and work performance. Following are ways to create a workplace in which discrimination-related problems are prevented or solved:

1. Make the library racially color blind by adopting/adhering to firm philosophies that communicate the commitment to employing individuals based solely on ability.

2. Hire and promote to management and supervisory positions only those persons with positive attitudes toward others.

3. Provide thorough and regular training on human relations, university hiring procedures, and legal issues relating to discrimination.

4. Make it clear to supervisors and managers that it is their job to ensure a discrimination-free workplace and that they are to confront and promptly resolve acts of discrimination, including jokes and harassment, and to investigate complaints and rumors.

5. Ensure that job descriptions are free of artificial barriers that might discriminate against protected groups and individuals.

6. Periodically review personnel policies in light of the potential for discrimination, particularly those relating to hiring, pay, promotions, benefits, and other practices that often give rise to discrimination, however unintentional.

7. Require that all personnel actions be centrally reviewed by a human resource professional or other knowledgeable person to ensure objectivity and consistency.

8. Consult with the university's human resources department to obtain advice and assistance on personnel actions prior to deciding or acting on them. Doing so is often a requirement.

9. If not already available, establish an administrative review procedure that encourages employees to take complaints to higher management.

10. Do not use race, color, national origin, or any other protected characteristic as a factor in any employment decision.

Performance Evaluations

THE PROBLEM. Everything appeared to Carolyn to be going smoothly enough. The circulation department was setting new highs each month for checkouts and for reserve materials use. The staff and student employees were working well together, and there was virtually no turnover. But that was about to change. Carolyn's thought turned to a memorandum from the dean's office reminding everyone that performance evaluations were due in 30 days. She sat at her desk and looked at her handwritten schedule. As in previous years she had asked each staff member to complete a self-evaluation for her. Then she had written a draft evaluation for each staff member, which was discussed in a meeting set up especially to discuss the draft. Together they finalized and signed the evaluations and turned them in to the library's personnel office. The evaluations were more of a nuisance than a useful process for Carolyn, except for this year. She had been planning for weeks to talk to Mark Gonzales about his work, and the process had presented a good opportunity to tell him that he needed to do a better job. Now Carolyn was looking at the stack of papers before her. The claim of discrimination from Mark Gonzales accusing her of singling him out because of his race was on her desk. Included in the packet were copies of the previous five evaluations, all giving Mark "superior" ratings for his work and the last one with two "needs improvement" ratings. Carolyn resolved then and there never to give anyone less than a "good" rating.

RESOLVING THE PROBLEM. Carolyn scheduled a meeting with the director of library personnel to make certain she understood all of the steps of the performance evaluation system and to review all of the steps she had taken with Mark. Carolyn, the director of library personnel, and the dean or dean designate would probably receive a series of questions or be interviewed by someone in the Equal Opportunity Programs Office regarding the complaint. More than likely the office would want to see what had been done in other similar situations (i.e., did other employees who were not Hispanic receive similar performance reviews)? What documentation was there that showed that the comments on the performance evaluation were justified? What evidence was there that Mark was being treated in a manner consistent with that of other employees?

All Carolyn could do at that point is wait for some response from the Equal Opportunity Programs Office regarding the complaint. She would also have to be sure that she didn't take any action against Mark that could be construed as retaliation.

PREVENTING THE PROBLEM. Documentation, documentation, documentation. Each action at every step of a progressive disciplinary process must be documented and copies provided to the employee. The performance evaluation system needs to be well documented and clearly understood by all involved and consistently applied to all employees. Do not wait until it's time to conduct the performance evaluation to take action relating to performance problems. Act when those problems are first evident. Maintain good communication with employees on a daily basis. No surprises.

Salary and Merit Determinations

THE PROBLEM. Although the library had done well in its annual campaign to raise acquisitions funds from private sources, the legislature had, before adjourning, approved only the smallest of salary indreases for librarians and staff. Along with the approval of raise monies came the directive to award all of the salary increase monies based on merit. After all, there were many in state employment who not only didn't deserve a raise but who, in truth, should be fired. The library was required to determine who would get awards of $495, $245, or $0 increases for the coming year. Dean Roberts wanted to just distribute what little money was available across the board. He knew that when there was not enough money for cost of living increases, merit increases destroyed morale. Naturally, the dean would await instructions from the provost, but he already knew that salary determinations would be difficult. He reviewed in his head the process for merit determination. Performance evaluations had already been completed; attached to each was a merit point recommendation made by the supervisor and department head. Based on those recommendations, the library's department heads would have to get together to agree on how to match those recommendations to the university provost's directions on the awarding of merit. As for the dean, he would only need to make some decisions on awarding merit to administrative staff as soon as the guidelines were agreed upon.

On the fourth day of September, Dean Roberts received official notification that he, the head of reference, and the desk supervisor in reference had been named in an equal pay suit by three women in the reference department. When analyzed, it was determined that the males in the library had received an average increase of $291 and the females had received an average increase of $248.

RESOLVING THE PROBLEM. If possible, Dean Roberts needs to meet with the individuals who have filed the complaint for the purpose of sharing relevant information with them. Although the statistical information may indeed point to a gender discrimination problem, it is assumed that the merit increases were determined in a fair, consistent manner. It is important that the individuals know how the salary increases were arrived at and by whom. If the individuals wish to continue their suit, all that Dean Roberts can do is make certain that he is confident in the decisions that were made, make adjustments if mistakes were made, and/or wait for the next step. This action will involve the university attorney's office, so it would be a good idea for Dean Roberts to arrange a preliminary meeting to discuss the issues.

PREVENTING THE PROBLEM. The library needs to develop merit criteria for both faculty and staff that are agreed upon by the relevant groups. Long before merit points are assigned, employees need to know the ground rules (i.e., in a merit system based on five points, everyone needs to understand what it will take to earn five points, four points, and so on). The best merit systems are tied in with the performance appraisal system with a schedule that calls for the performance evaluations to be completed just before merit points are decided. Ideally, employees would know at the beginning of the year what is expected of them, what it will take to earn highest merit, and the schedule for completion of appraisals and assignment of merit. If merit is assigned based on performance, there should be few disagreements, and if there appears to be inequity based on gender, it can be explained.

Dealing with Poor Performance

THE PROBLEM. Frank had just returned from the dean's office where they had discussed the problem he had. Actually, *the problem* had begun more than nine months before when his unit head had talked with him about Martha's work. Martha had barely passed her probationary period, and Frank wished now that they had terminated her then. Now, Jean, the unit head, wanted to fire Martha. Jean and Frank had discussed the procedure with the head of library personnel and had agreed to take specific actions with regard to Martha. Her job was to check in new serials on the automated system and to make sure that all of the periodicals were correctly marked and shelved. Jean had assigned an additional student assistant to Martha, but the work still was not getting done correctly. Jean and Frank had established performance standards for all of the jobs in the serials receiving unit. Martha was unable to meet the standards. They had provided Martha with additional training and had personally verified that she knew how to do the work. They were faced with the only decision they could make—to terminate her employment. Both of them knew that they needed to give Martha a formal verbal warning, followed by a written warning if things didn't improve. The termination letter was delivered to Martha in May. All of these actions were taken with the knowledge and approval of the dean, the personnel librarian, and the human resources department. It was now November. Martha's position had been posted and filled. Her replacement, Theresa, was doing a great job. Although it did not concern him greatly, Frank knew that he and the dean as well as other staff members in the library would be involved in responding to the discrimination claim before him. Martha was claiming that she had been fired in violation of the Americans with Disabilities Act because she had an attention deficit disorder and no accommodations had been made by the library.

RESOLVING THE PROBLEM. Jean and Frank both knew that the first questions that needed answers were (1) Did Martha inform the library that she had a disability? and (2) Was an accommodation needed to allow her to do the work? A disabled individual, for the purposes of the law, is a person who has a physical or mental impairment that limits one or more major life activities, has a record of such impairment, or is regarded by others as showing such an impairment.[2] Impairments that limit major life activities must be substantial as opposed to minor and include impairments that, among others, limit learning—thus, an individual with a learning disability would be covered. If Martha had notified the library of an attention deficit disorder, classed as a learning disability, a reasonable accommodation might include additional training designed to most appropriately meet the preferred learning style of the employee. For example, if Martha learns best by having a task explained and then performing that task repeatedly with the trainer observing her performance, then that method should be tried. If she does not learn well when the trainer hands her written instructions, that method should be avoided. In consultation with the Equal Opportunity Programs Office, the library could have made reasonable accommodations.

If Martha had indeed notified the library of her disability and the library knew an accommodation was needed, Martha was correct in her suit. If she did not notify anyone, the termination would probably stand. Jean and Frank talked with the personnel librarian and the dean and determined that all they could do is wait to see if they would need to respond. The dean was in touch with the university counsel's office and the Equal Opportunity Programs Office about the situation.

PREVENTING THE PROBLEM. Make certain that all managers in the library understand the provisions of the Americans with Disabilities Act (ADA). Any employee who wishes to inform the library of a disability should be referred to the library's personnel office, who should know exactly how to address the issue. Provide library faculty and staff with training sessions on ADA.

Reassignment

THE PROBLEM. Francis had been the library's personnel specialist for the past seven years and was a tenured associate professor in the library. During those seven years, she had worked closely with approximately 15 reassignments of librarians and staff from one department to another within the library system. It was the library's unwritten practice to try to find a good match between individual and position if at all possible. Some reassignments were of the type where an individual is an outstanding performer but wants a new challenge. Others were of the type where an individual had become a problem in one department but was believed to be able to contribute in another department. Another type of situation was when an individual was a poor performer who needed a second chance to prove himself or herself. Francis was generally very pleased with the results of most reassignments. There were at least 10 individuals in jobs in which they excelled because of the library's reassignment practices. Unfortunately, she held in her hand the paperwork related to a reassignment where the individual was not excelling. William had been hired as the night supervisor in the geology library. He had been involved in several incidents where student employees had complained about his supervisory skills.

Francis and the head of the geology library had worked out a reassignment for William to the acquisitions department. It was a lateral move to a job of the same level but without supervisory responsibilities. The head of acquisitions had given William adequate training, and he had proven he knew how to do the work. However, staff in the department had complained to their supervisor that William was spending all of his time on the phone and that they were having to do his work. Couldn't they also share his paycheck? William's supervisor had followed the procedures to the letter. Verbal warning, written warning, and then she was prepared to terminate William after he returned from vacation. William did not return. On Francis's desk was an unemployment claim for William who said he was the victim of constructive discharge and was going to sue for back pay and damages. He claimed that he had been moved from the job he was hired for and that the library had changed his working conditions so they could fire him.

RESOLVING THE PROBLEM. Again, documentation, documentation, documentation. Francis knew she needed to work with the dean to make sure all of the documentation was in order. The documentation would include the library's and the university's approved reassignment policies and an accounting of what actions were taken when, by whom, and how. Francis also knew that if the case went very far at all, she would be asked to document how other employees were reassigned—when, by whom, and how. She knew that if she could show that other employees were treated the same way, the library would be found to have acted correctly.

PREVENTING THE PROBLEM. It is essential that if employees are going to be reassigned within the library, there be an approved reassignment policy and that it be applied consistently. The dean probably will have the authority to reassign librarians within the library (because they retain their faculty status no matter where they work in the library) but may face more restrictions when it comes to reassigning staff (because they are normally hired into a specific grade and position title). Because of the specificity of staff assignments, moving them can be more difficult. You don't want to create a problem by moving an individual to a higher position (which might take away promotional opportunities for other staff) or to a lower position (which probably requires demotion and lower pay).

Discipline

THE PROBLEM. When Allen was hired as team leader in the catalog department, he knew there were a few unresolved personnel issues. One he was vaguely familiar with had to do with Diane, who had been transferred to another department. Apparently what had happened was that Diane was having difficulty dealing with the many changes in the department and had been unable to keep up with her coworkers in terms of the number of books done and in keeping errors to a minimum. Diane was transferred against her will; she believed she was capable of doing the work and had simply not been trained adequately. The department head argued that she had received not only the same training as others but had been given additional training, yet she was still making too many errors. Diane was first reassigned to other tasks in the department that had previously been handled by student workers. Then she was transferred to another department with the intent of training her to do work at her level. Allen was now looking over the paperwork. There were several performance evaluations and letters detailing the problems Diane had been having in the catalog department. Then there was the most recent performance evaluation, done by his predecessor, with a glowing evaluation of Diane's work. It looked like she had been doing very good work in the past year and that she had been transferred without cause. He knew that she had been given both verbal and written warnings about her work in her new department. He expected to learn any day that she had been terminated. But now he had a positive evaluation which she would certainly use to argue unfair treatment. Might Diane be coming back to his unit?

RESOLVING THE PROBLEM. This situation points out the need for consistent application of the performance evaluation system. The first thing anyone will look at are the previous performance evaluations. If they are good and then suddenly bad, there is a problem. All Allen could do is try to explain, in the form of a memo to the file with a copy to the employee, why the last evaluation was inaccurate. Then he would have to wait to see if there was to be any further action taken by the employee.

PREVENTING THE PROBLEM. Everyone who writes performance evaluations needs to understand how to do them properly. The standards established on which performance is based have to be applied consistently to all of the staff who are to meet or exceed those standards. In this litigious society, more and more employers are being sued by employees and former employees; therefore, it is important to be aware of what is legal and permissible in appraising employee performance. The key to making nondiscriminatory appraisals is quite simple: Evaluate all employees on the basis of job performance only, be consistent in application, and apply criteria objectively to all employees. Evaluating employees on the basis of job performance means judging them only on the way they do their jobs without regard to their age, race, sex, religion, or national origin. It also means putting aside any personal likes or dislikes. Good evaluation focuses on the standards of performance and not on personality, lessening the possibility of discrimination.

Personal Problems

THE PROBLEM. Joan hadn't seen the item in the paper, but a friend informed her in the parking lot about what had happened. In addition, one of the library specialists in her department cut the story from the newspaper and left it on Joan's desk. Susan's former live-in boyfriend had been arrested the previous night for domestic violence against her. He had barricaded himself in her house, threatening to shoot anyone who came close. The police had rushed the house, shooting him in the leg in the process. Susan was not at work but had confided to a coworker that she feared for her life when he was released. Susan's life had been turned upside down, but Joan had to consider the library and the work for which Susan was responsible. She knew that everything could be handled for a week or two, but Susan was badly needed to work her night and weekend hours. The department was already having difficulty maintaining its coverage. What role did the library have in giving Susan the protection she felt she needed? What accommodations could or should the library make for her? What kind of balance is there between helping Susan and getting the work done? No doubt Susan could use her annual leave and probably get some leave without pay if needed, but what about the department's schedule? Susan had already requested to be excused from night shifts because she was afraid of her estranged boyfriend. How much should Susan's personal difficulties be allowed to affect the department's services?

RESOLVING THE PROBLEM. Joan contacted the library's personnel office and reviewed the leave without pay policy with the director. The policy would permit Susan to request leave without pay for personal reasons and would require that she stipulate the dates of the leave, understanding that her insurance coverage would be affected. Joan knew that Susan really could not afford to take leave without pay but wanted to be sure she knew the procedure. Joan also contacted the campus police to ascertain whether or not they could provide an escort for Susan to and from the parking lot, and whether or not Susan or a coworker could call them for assistance if the ex-boyfriend showed up. The campus police informed Joan that Susan would have to make the initial contact but that they appreciated knowing about the situation and would be alert to potential problems. Clearly, the library would assist in ensuring Susan's safety at work and while on campus but could go no further.

PREVENTING THE PROBLEM. Little could be done to prevent the problems in this instance because they were completely beyond the scope of the job and the reach of the employer. The library and its staff can provide the employee with support and encouragement. Those working with Susan need to know the situation but should not do anything that would interfere with the police department's handling of the case. Knowledge of the university's policies and the campus police services would be very useful for the manager.

Workplace Problem Resolution

It is important to remember that the suggestions offered in these scenarios are not absolute answers. The situations, circumstances, and the people involved differ from one problem to another. You will have to evaluate each instance individually and decide what course of action would be the most appropriate. Know your limitations. Your advice or answers may do more to complicate the problem than solve it for the employee. Remember that you are not alone. Seek the advice of your supervisor or fellow employee supervisors, keeping in mind that no one may have had precisely the same problem with the same circumstances. Consult the numerous books on supervision that are available. Mix in all you learn from colleagues and books with a large dose of common sense and humaneness and you will do fine.

References

1. Lewin G. Joel III, *Every Employee's Guide to the Law: Everything You Need to Know About Your Rights in the Workplace—And What to Do If They Are Violated* (New York: Pantheon, 1993), 6.

2. *Americans with Disabilities Act of 1990* (PL 101-336, 26 July 1990), 104 *United States Statutes at Large:* 331.

Bibliography

Belton, Robert. *Remedies in Employment Discrimination Law.* New York: Wiley Law Publications, 1992.

Elias, Stephen. *Legal Research: How to Find and Understand the Law.* Berkeley, Calif.: Nolo Press, 1995.

Gilberg, Kenneth R. "Employers Must Protect Their Companies Against Employee Lawsuits." *Supervision, The Magazine of Industrial Relations* 53, no. 11 (November 1992): 12.

"How to Avoid Discrimination Suits." *Nation's Business* 80, no. 3 (March 1992): 46.

Laabs, Jennifer J. "Remedies for HR's Legal Headache." *Personnel Journal* 73, no. 12 (December 1994): 66.

Merkel, Muriel. *Your Rights as an Employee: How Federal Labor Laws Protect Workers in Private Employment*. New York: Vanguard Press, 1985.

Osigweh, Chimezie A.B., ed. *Managing Employee Rights and Responsibilities*. New York: Quorum Books, 1989.

Rothstein, Mark A., and Lance Liebman. *Cases and Materials on Employment Law*, 3rd ed. Westbury, N.Y.: Foundation Press, 1994.

Ruzicho, Andrew J., and Louis A. Jacobs. *Employment Practices Manual: A Guide to Minimizing Constitutional, Statutory, and Common-Law Liability*. Deerfield, Ill.: Clark Boardman Callaghan, 1994.

Schoorman, F. David, and Matthew V. Champagne. "Managers as Informal Third Parties: The Impact of Supervisor-Subordinate Relationships on Interventions." *Employee Responsibilities and Rights Journal* 7, no. 1 (March 1994): 73.

■■■■■■ Conclusion

Sound Library Management

Always do right; this will gratify
some people and astonish the rest.
Samuel Langhorne Clemens (1835-1910)

Although the primary focus of this book is on employer/employee rights and responsibilities, some discussion of good management is desirable. This conclusion deals with very real situations in libraries. Although most librarians are not trained as supervisors, managers, or administrators, today's large libraries are complex organizations with multimillion dollar budgets, employing hundreds of individuals. These libraries require skilled and knowledgeable management. The following information is aimed at creating an awareness of good practices, which, along with an understanding of employer/employee rights and responsibilities, will help the good manager become a better one.

The Reluctant Manager

In many organizations, including libraries, a primary means of advancement involves assuming supervisory, managerial, or administrative responsibilities. The nature of one's job is often dramatically transformed by the new tasks, the skills for which are not obtained automatically with the new responsibilities. One result is that good librarians or good staff can become mediocre or bad managers and unhappy library employees with only slightly larger paychecks. Consider Maryanne's situation.

133

Maryanne couldn't wait to complete the Master's Degree in Library Science program so she could go to work. After some serious thought, she had decided that she wanted to work in an academic library, probably a small college library. She was successful in getting the first position she applied for at a small four-year school nearby. In retrospect, she wished that she had asked a few more questions during the interview. The job was not exactly what was advertised. The library was so short staffed that shortly after learning everyone's name, Maryanne was assigned the supervision of the four clerical workers and two other librarians. Although she had the least seniority and was by far the youngest librarian, the others just didn't want to supervise anyone. Neither did the head librarian.

Maryanne loved her work and had good relationships with her coworkers, but she was completely unprepared to tackle supervisory responsibilities. Seven months to the day after receiving her M.A.L.S., Maryanne decided to quit after an unpleasant meeting with the head librarian in which she refused to consider changing Maryanne's duties. Maryanne was frustrated by the fact that there were no clear objectives for the library and there were problems that no one knew how to address. All of the librarians and staff members loved books and all provided excellent service to the students and faculty, but none of them had a clue about library management.

Shortly after making her decision, Maryanne was hired by an ARL library to work in its catalog department. Four months after Maryanne started work, the team leader of the general cataloging group resigned. Following a number of closed door meetings, Maryanne was made team leader of general cataloging. She learned later that no one else wanted the responsibility. She also learned that the other staff members were all making more money than she. Although it was never clear why, the department head was yelling at her every day. The department head didn't want to be a manager either and shouldn't have been. Everyone was just waiting for an opportunity to have him removed. Maryanne tried to be a good manager, but there was no support, no training, and no incentive. After trying without success to transfer to the reference department, Maryanne left the ARL library before her tenure review. Not wanting to move again, Maryanne took a part-time job at the public library and a full-time job at an insurance company. Now she could do reference work and claims adjustment without having to manage or supervise anyone but herself.

Maryanne's experiences may be a bit extreme, but in some libraries, the librarians shy away from managerial responsibilities and often a reluctant librarian is thrust into a supervisory role. Many, if not most, librarians choose their profession because of their desire to serve the public by organizing and making information available to users. Generally, librarians want to provide access to collections. Few chose librarianship because of its opportunities to manage people as well as collections. Consequently, few librarians have adequate training to be effective managers. But librarians are not alone—in academia, outstanding professors are often encouraged to become department heads and deans just as outstanding librarians are encouraged to fill administrative positions because that is where higher salaries are to be found.

The Complex Organization

As H. L. Mencken said, "For every complex problem there's a simple answer, and it's wrong." The library is a very complex organization; thus it is difficult to make generalizations. Academic libraries differ from public and special libraries, and large academic libraries differ not only from small college libraries but also from each other in many respects.

The library is an organization composed of individuals who often have little in common except their training in library science and a desire to serve. By its nature, the library needs individuals trained in various subject areas for its subject libraries and its subject cataloging. The library needs individuals who are detail-oriented for developing access tools for collections and individuals who are people-oriented for its public services. It requires administrators who are able to deal not only with multimillion dollar budgets but also with several hundred individuals on the payroll. The accountants and catalogers in the library want and need hard and fast rules while the branch heads, personnel specialists, and reference staff want to be able to fit the rules to the situation when necessary.

Human resources management in libraries is not an exact science that presents clear alternatives that are either right or wrong. When it is clear some action must be taken, often choices must be made from among alternatives, none of which are particularly attractive. Librarians are often torn between doing things right and doing the right things. Libraries are complex organizations, and human resources management is complex because people are complex. Although some employees may be anxious to participate in decisionmaking, other employees would rather not take the risk or assume any additional responsibility or make any changes. In libraries, as in all organizations, are employees who are unable or unwilling to do the assigned work. Managers, in order to be effective, must be able to improve the work of poor performers.

Definitions

The tendency among librarians is to use management terms interchangeably. There is often discussion about managers, supervisors, and administrators that implies that they are all the same, and when we speak of personnel administration, paper shufflers and bureaucrats come to mind. So before we begin any discussion about human resources management and library managers, supervisors, and administrators, let's define the terms.

Supervision

According to the Taft-Hartley Act of 1947, "anyone at the first level of management who has the responsibility for getting the 'hands-on-the-work' employees to carry out the plans and policies of higher level management is a supervisor."[1] The Taft-Hartley Act of 1947 defines a supervisor as "any individual having authority, in the interest of the employer, to hire, transfer, suspend, lay off, recall, promote, discharge, assign, reward, or discipline other employees, or responsibility to direct them, or to adjust their grievances, or effectively to recommend such action, if in connection with the foregoing the exercise of such authority is not of a merely routine or clerical nature, but requires the use of independent judgement."[2]

The word *supervisor* derives from a Latin term meaning to "look over." Early on, the supervisor was the person in charge of a group of workers and was a foreman or "fore man," at the lead of a group, setting the pace for the rest. Today's supervisor is a leader, one who watches over the work, and a person with technical and professional skills.

Management

The most common definition of management is "getting things done through other people." The primary task of any employee is "getting things done." As a staff member, getting things done is the most important part of the job. Because it is clear that there is more work than one person can accomplish, it is necessary to use additional employees to do the work. Therefore, as a manager, you must not only accomplish your own work, but you must get things done through other workers.

Doing a job and getting someone else to do it are entirely different. Simply telling someone to do something right very seldom works. The employee must be motivated to do it right as well as have the prerequisite knowledge and skills. If the work is not done right, it is the manager's responsibility to teach and apply supervisory techniques that will allow the employee to do things right.

Every employee has different needs, skills, attitudes, and motivations. The manager needs to deal with each employee differently while dealing with all employees fairly. There is no universal technique that will work with every employee. What works today with one employee may have no effect tomorrow, and what works on one worker may have a completely negative effect on another worker.

Administration

One dimension of managerial performance is administration. The manager has to administer—to manage and improve what already exists. Administration involves focusing on improving the efficiency and effectiveness of existing programs and services by directing resources to areas of need. Efficiency focuses on costs, while effectiveness focuses on opportunity. The good administrator determines what resources and efforts are to be allocated so as to produce desired results. Library administration is focused in the director's office, which must be responsive not only to the internal needs of the library but also to the needs of the library's customers and administrative superiors.

The Supervisor, Manager, and Administrator

Because each has distinct functions, the terms are not interchangeable, although on any given day each performs some of the duties of the other. For the purposes of this book, the manager and administrator terms are used interchangeably because we deal primarily with the personnel/human resources person who is a manager or administrator.

Managing in a Complex Environment

Generally, librarians, not unlike other university faculty, are minimally prepared to manage people. At one time or another, we've all come face to face with an ineffective library manager: the overcontroller, who believes that it is necessary to show everyone who is boss; the undercontroller, who refuses to make decisions in an attempt to make everyone happy; the poor communicator, who gives orders without listening or just listens without providing leadership; and the poor delegator, who either delegates responsibility without the authority to act or simply refuses to delegate at all. Much can be learned from reviewing those traits that employees like least about their managers:

1. *Too sensitive.* Employees don't like to have to tiptoe around their managers for fear of upsetting them or saying the wrong thing if they are in a bad mood or take everything personally.

2. *Indecisive.* Indecisive managers can survive in an organization but will not win the support of employees.

3. *Overly opinionated.* Managers who will not listen to any kind of reasoning but always have their minds made up will find that employees will soon stop making suggestions.

4. *Autocratic.* Managers must understand that if they do not allow their employees to participate in decisions, a lot of good talent will be wasted.

5. *Uses vulgar language.* Crude language impresses no one and must be avoided at all costs.

6. *Has an unstable personality.* Employees shouldn't have to guess which manager came to work that day. Unpredictable changes in a manager's personality cause problems.

7. *Dishonest.* Managers need to recognize the importance of honesty in the workplace and make it easy for employees to be honest.

8. *Shows favoritism.* Even if other employees are treated fairly, they resent it if another employee is given more favorable treatment. Problems like this may lead to discrimination charges, even though in most cases prejudice is not involved.

9. *Does not listen.* Good managers are anxious to hear what employees think about the job and encourage employees to provide feedback. Nothing is more frustrating than to talk to a manager who does not listen.

10. *Can't accept bad news.* Managers must be willing to listen to bad news and not punish the messenger. It won't take long for employees to realize that the manager wants to hear only good news and that problems that need attention will be ignored.

11. *Ridicules employees.* A manager who ridicules or makes sarcastic remarks to employees may not even realize it. Ridiculing an employee in front of peers is unforgivable. Managers must be aware of how their words affect employees. Managers must be tactful.

12. *Makes uninformed decisions.* Employees respect managers who make decisions based on information.

13. *Mistrusts employees.* The manager must trust employees, and the employees must be able to trust their manager.

14. *Makes impossible promises.* Employees know when the manager makes promises that cannot be kept. The manager's credibility is destroyed if this happens often.

15. *Breaks reasonable promises.* Employees also know when the manager's promises can be kept and are not. Managers must keep to their word or be able to explain why a promise is not kept.

16. *Does not manage time well.* Managers with poor time management skills will waste their employees' time as well as their own.

17. *Is disorganized.* Employees want a manager who is organized and can get things done.

18. *Fails to exert authority.* Employees respect managers who know how to use their authority. Employees want a leader.

19. *Is a poor planner.* The manager who fails to plan anything in advance wastes employees' time. Poorly planned meetings, for example, are terrible time wasters.

20. *Communicates poorly.* Managers must develop good communication skills.

Why Managers Fail

In addition to all of the things a manager can do wrong, the individual's managerial style may be a cause of failure. Managerial styles cover the full spectrum, from laissez-faire to authoritarian. The manager who lacks self-confidence or feels uncomfortable in the managerial role tends to let the unit run itself. The dictatorial or authoritarian manager tends to oversupervise. Most good managers are found in the middle of the spectrum. When a manager doesn't succeed you must look at the specific situation to determine the exact reasons. It is possible that the failure can be traced to lack of support from the boss or lack of training or encouragement. Most failures, however, can be attributed to one of the following six managerial pitfalls:

1. Poor personal relations with employees, top management, or fellow managers.

2. Lack of initiative or emotional stability.

3. Unwillingness or inability to understand the management point of view.

4. Failure to spend the necessary effort or time to improve skills.

5. Lack of skill in planning and organizing the work of other employees.

6. Unwillingness or inability to adjust to changing conditions.

Problems Faced by New Managers

One of the biggest problems facing new managers is their lack of preparation for the job. In libraries, an individual is often selected for promotion to a management position because of performance as a specialist. Those skills and abilities are often quite different from those needed by a manager. Organizations normally expect new managers to step into the job and function right away. This expectation exists even though statistics show that most organizations offer little help or support to them. Often, formal managerial training is not provided to the new manager until after six to twelve months on the job. The "sink or swim" philosophy prevails. In addition, the new manager often lacks an immediate peer group. Former peers no longer regard the new manager as one of them. Other managers are hesitant to consider this person a part of their group until he or she has demonstrated the ability to think and act like management. This leaves the new manager with no one at a time when support from others is badly needed. The administration needs to recognize that it takes time for new managers to become effective and that they need help and support. The process of becoming a good manager is an ongoing process—one that never stops.

Expectations for Managers

Supervising people is undoubtedly the most difficult and complex activity of managers who are the direct link between the administrative structure and the operational structure of an organization. To employees, the manager represents "the organization." Workers' feelings about the organization, management, and their jobs are directly affected by their relationships with their immediate supervisors. The administration's assessment of a unit's effectiveness is based on worker productivity, which has a direct impact on the organization's ability to meet its goals. Many people in technical and staff positions fail to recognize or appreciate the demands placed on managers. Medical research has shown that managerial positions carry with them tremendous stress. Although it is true that some people work better under stress and find that channeling stress into productive activity can be satisfying, stress can also contribute to heart attacks, ulcers, and medical depression. To be able to successfully supervise requires considerable training and skill development.

Personal Qualities of Good Managers

Having established that librarians often don't choose librarianship because of the opportunity to manage people, that preparation is sparse, that there are lots of things employees don't like about their managers, and that managers make a variety of mistakes in managing, what are the personal qualities of good managers?

1. *Energy and good health.* Managing is a demanding activity and requires that individuals not only be able to handle a variety of activities but be physically and emotionally up to the task.

2. *Leadership potential.* Managerial responsibilities require the ability to get people to work for and with you to accomplish the objectives of your unit.

3. *Ability to get along with people.* One of the most important qualities library administrators look for in a manager is the ability to get along with others. Getting others to carry out their responsibilities depends greatly on their feelings toward their manager.

4. *Job know-how and technical competence.* The manager must know the job in order to be effective in training and problem solving. Managers in libraries usually have their own job duties and responsibilities in addition to supervision and must be proficient in those duties.

5. *Initiative.* The manager needs to be able to recognize when adjustments must be made in the work flow or changes made in order to improve procedures. Initiative is required in order to be aware when potential problems loom and when problems occur.

6. *Dedication and dependability.* Workers who sense that their manager is not dedicated to the job and employer will display the same attitude. For example, a manager who is absent regularly will find that employees will also be absent regularly.

7. *Positive attitude toward the library's administration.* Workers will mirror the feelings of the manager.

Types of Persons Who Should Not Be Managers

There are definitely certain types of persons to avoid when filling managerial positions. If selecting a person from your staff, avoid the negative employee, the rigid employee, the unproductive employee, and the disgruntled employee. The attitude of a negative employee will be contagious among employees. The rigid employee will be unable to deal effectively with employees. The unproductive employee will find it difficult to get others to work hard. The disgruntled employee will infect others with his or her negative feelings.

Manager Attitudes

Attitude is extremely important to good supervision. Managers have the proper attitude if they agree with the following statements:

1. Managers must manage with a high degree of integrity and lead by example.

2. Managers must keep their word to employees.

3. Managers must earn the respect, trust, and confidence of employees.

4. Managers must strive to help employees develop to their full potential.

5. Managers must give credit to employees who do a good job.

6. Managers must accept higher level decisions and directives and support them to employees.

7. Managers must refrain from discussing personal feelings about library administration with employees.

8. Managers must discuss disagreements with library administration privately.

9. Managers must be responsible for the performance of their employees.

10. Managers must be objective in judging the actions of employees.

11. Managers must decide matters involving employees on the bases of facts and circumstances, not personal sympathies.

12. Managers must accept the responsibility for rehabilitating rather than punishing employees whenever possible.

13. Managers must be prepared to support employees in cases where they are in the right.

14. Managers must allow employees to have as much control over their own work as possible.

15. Managers must work to maintain a climate in the workplace that allows employees to express their feelings and concerns openly without fear of reprisal.

The Library Manager

Individuals, whether charged with the responsibility of supervising one student or twenty-five librarians, need essentially the same basic supervisory skills. We tend to underestimate the value and impact of student employee supervision. On the one hand, it can provide valuable supervisory experience, which can prepare one for higher level supervision if done well. On the other hand, if done poorly, it can have a very negative effect on students, for many of whom this is a first job. Libraries must pay attention to the fact that assigning supervisory responsibilities to an individual carries with it the obligation to help him or her learn and develop good supervisory skills.

A Great Place to Work

Just how good an employer is your library? How can you measure it? Robert Levering, in his book *A Great Place to Work*, says, "From an employee viewpoint, a great workplace is one in which you trust the people you work for, have pride in what you do, and enjoy the people you are working with."[3] Libraries should consider whether or not they are "great workplaces" according to this definition. One of the most important, and most difficult, tasks for administrators and managers is to create an environment of trust in an organization. Levering[4] recommends that employers demonstrate their trustworthiness by:

practicing patience and consistency;

implementing and changing their policies and practices with care and deliberateness;

being open and accessible;

being willing to do more than they have to for employees;

delivering on their promises; and

sharing the credit and the rewards of a job well done with their employees.

In doing all of the above, employers can demonstrate that they are acting in good faith and that they respect employees as people. If libraries act in good faith, according to this definition, they can develop strong employer/employee relationships that benefit all concerned.

Employees are concerned with the quality of work life and want greater participation in library decision making. Many of today's library employees want a higher level of involvement in their jobs and want the opportunity to make a greater contribution to the organization. Many library directors recognize the contributions staff can make through participation in decision making and are finding ways of involving library employees. That involvement enriches jobs and makes them more satisfying and challenging, resulting in a better workplace.

We in libraries would like to think that we are good employers and provide employees with a good, if not great, workplace. An understanding of employer/employee rights and responsibilities will help library managers work toward that goal—providing a great place to work.

References

1. *Labor Management Relations Act of 1947* (PL 61-120, 23 June 1947), 61 *United States Statutes at Large:* 138.

2. Ibid.

3. Robert Levering, *A Great Place to Work* (New York: Random House, 1988), 26.

4. Ibid., 45.

Bibliography

Argyris, Chris. *Integrating the Individual and the Organization*. New York: Wiley, 1964.

Boaz, Martha, ed. *Current Concepts in Library Management*. Littleton, Colo.: Libraries Unlimited, 1979.

Dougherty, Richard M., and Fred J. Heinritz. *Scientific Management of Library Operations.*, 2nd ed. Metuchen, N.J.: Scarecrow Press, 1982.

Drucker, Peter F. *The Effective Executive*. New York: Harper & Row, 1966.

————. *Managing for Results*. New York: Harper & Row, 1964.

————. *Managing the Non-Profit Organization: Practices and Principles*. New York: Harper & Row, 1990.

Durey, Peter. *Staff Management in University and College Libraries*. Oxford: Pergamon Press, 1976.

Evans, G. Edward. *Management Techniques for Librarians*, 2nd ed. New York: Academic Press, 1983.

Frierson, James G. *Preventing Employment Lawsuits: An Employer's Guide to Hiring, Discipline, and Discharge*. Washington, D.C.: Bureau of National Affairs, 1994.

Gilbreth, Frank B., Jr., and Ernestine Gilbreth Casey. *Cheaper by the Dozen*. New York: Crowell, 1948.

Glaviano, Cliff, and R. Errol Lam. "Academic Libraries and Affirmative Action: Approaching Cultural Diversity in the 1990's." *College and Research Libraries* 51, no. 6 (1992): 513.

Gould, William B. *Agenda for Reform: The Future of Employment Relationships and the Law*. Cambridge, Mass.: MIT Press, 1993.

Guyton, Theodore L. *Unionization: The Viewpoint of Librarians*. Chicago: American Library Association, 1975.

Hunsaker, Phillip L. *The Art of Managing People*. Englewood Cliffs, N.J.: Prentice-Hall, 1980.

Kusack, James M. *Unions for Academic Library Support Staff: Impact on Workers and Workplace*. Westport, Conn.: Greenwood Press, 1986.

Likert, Rensis. *The Human Organization: Its Management and Value*. New York: McGraw-Hill, 1967.

Lyle, Guy R. *The Administration of the College Library*, 4th ed. New York: H.W. Wilson, 1974.

Lynch, Beverly, ed. *The Academic Library in Transition: Planning for the 1990s*. New York: Neal-Schuman, 1989.

Lynch, Beverly, ed. *Management Strategies for Libraries: A Basic Reader*. New York: Neal-Schuman, 1985.

Marchant, Maurice P. *Participative Management in Academic Libraries*. Westport, Conn.: Greenwood Press, 1976.

Martell, Charles. *The Client-Centered Academic Library: An Organizational Model*. Westport, Conn.: Greenwood Press, 1986.

Martin, Lowell A. *Organizational Structure of Libraries*. Metuchen, N.J.: Scarecrow Press, 1984.

Martin, Murray S. *Financial Planning for Libraries*. New York: Haworth, 1983.

McCabe, Gerard B., ed. *The Smaller Academic Library: A Management Handbook*. Westport, Conn.: Greenwood Press, 1986.

Parkinson, C. Northcote. *Parkinson's Law and Other Studies in Administration*. Boston: Houghton-Mifflin, 1957.

Peter, Laurence J. *The Peter Principle*. New York: Morrow, 1969.

Peters, Tom. *Thriving on Chaos*. New York: Knopf, 1987.

Prentice, Ann E. *Financial Planning for Libraries*. Metuchen, N.J.: Scarecrow Press, 1983.

Rizzo, John R. *Management for Librarians: Fundamentals and Issues*. Westport, Conn.: Greenwood Press, 1980.

Rogers, Rutherford D., and David C. Weber. *University Library Administration*. New York: Wilson, 1971.

Stueart, Robert D., and Barbara B. Moran. *Library Management*, 3rd ed. Littleton, Colo.: Libraries Unlimited, 1987.

Weatherford, John W. *Collective Bargaining and the Academic Librarian*. Metuchen, N.J.: Scarecrow Press, 1976.

—————. *Librarians' Agreements: Bargaining for a Heterogeneous Profession*. Metuchen, N.J.: Scarecrow Press, 1988.

White, Herbert S. *Managing the Special Library*. White Plains, N.Y.: Knowledge Industry Publications, 1984.

▌▌▌▌▌▌ Glossary

He who wishes to know the road
through the mountains must ask
those who have already trodden it.

Chinese Proverb

This book, written by a librarian for other librarians, contains many legal terms that may or may not be familiar to the reader. The following glossary presents those terms with brief definitions as they relate to employment.

ADA: *See* Americans with Disabilities Act.

ADEA: *See* Age Discrimination in Employment Act.

Administrative remedy: A claim made through a governmental agency, such as the Equal Employment Opportunity Commission of the Department of Labor, as opposed to a claim pursued through the courts.

Adverse impact: A negative effect, as in work rules that have an adverse impact on people who, because of historic class discrimination, are given extra protections by laws that prohibit discrimination based on race, ethnicity, religion, sex, age, or disability.

Affirmative action: A hiring policy requiring employers to analyze their workforce for underuse of protected-class individuals and to develop a plan of action to correct that problem if it exists; managerial strategies designed to enhance racial, ethnic, and gender diversity in the workplace through hiring, training, and promoting of minorities.

Age Discrimination in Employment Act: Designed to protect people age 40 and over from discharge or discipline based on their age.

Agency shop: A clause in a collective bargaining agreement that requires nonunion members to pay the union an amount equal to the amount of members' dues; in other words, agency shop employees do not have to belong to the union but in effect have to pay union dues.

Americans with Disabilities Act (ADA): Passed in 1986, this law is designed to protect disabled individuals from employment discrimination. It requires employers to offer reasonable accommodation of their disability and also sets standards for public access (i.e., making buildings and services accessible to persons with disabilities).

Assumption of the risk: A legal theory that states that an individual who is aware of the hazards of an activity but engages in that activity nevertheless cannot recover damages if he or she is injured by the hazard.

Back pay: A damage award in a lawsuit allowing recovery of wages an employee would have earned if he or she had not been illegally fired or denied a promotion, for example.

Base period: The minimum period of working time required to qualify for unemployment compensation benefits.

Base period wages: The minimum amount of base period earnings required to qualify for unemployment compensation benefits.

Blacklisting: Circulating or publishing a person's name with the intention of interfering with his or her chances for employment.

Bona fide occupation qualification (BFOQ): A normally discriminatory job requirement that is legitimate under specific circumstances (e.g., seeking only female candidates for a female acting role).

Bottom-line test: A comparison of actual hiring rates, rather than selection methods, to determine whether or not hiring practices have an adverse impact on members of a protected group.

Boycott: A refusal to work for or patronize an employer with whom a union is involved in a labor dispute.

Burden of proof: The obligation placed by the court on a specific party to establish a case.

Business necessity/justification: A valid economic reason for an employer to make an employment decision; for example, a loss of customers may cause a business necessity or be a sufficient business justification for layoffs.

Casual employee: A worker who performs a job that is not within the scope of the employer's usual business, such as a person who cleans carpet in a dentist's office.

Causal connection: A link between events that is close enough to establish a cause-and-effect relationship.

Chain of custody: The course taken by a blood or urine sample between its donor and its analysis, which must be guarded to ensure the integrity of the sample.

Civil lawsuit: A lawsuit brought by one individual or entity against another, as opposed to a criminal lawsuit, which is brought by the government against an individual or entity.

Class action: A lawsuit undertaken by one or more members of an aggrieved group on behalf of all of its members.

Closed shop: An agreement between a union and an employer whereby the employer agrees to hire only union members; closed shops are illegal under the Taft-Hartley Act.

COBRA: The Consolidated Omnibus Budget Reconciliation Act, which gives terminated employees the right to continuation of health insurance coverage at group rates, usually for up to 18 months.

Company union: A union supported by and effectively controlled by an employer, either financially or otherwise.

Comparable worth: A theory that people doing different jobs of roughly equal worth to their employer should be paid the same wage, regardless of sex. Comparable worth is an extension of the Equal Pay Act, which requires equal pay for equal work.

Compensatory damages: Damages awarded by a court to repay an individual for losses suffered (e.g., lost wages and benefits, pain and suffering, and emotional stress).

Compensatory time: Time off given to employees in lieu of overtime; also known as "comp time." Compensatory time is generally not allowed for private employers under the Fair Labor Standards Act.

Conflict of laws: Laws, usually one state and one federal, that impose different requirements in similar circumstances. Employers must follow the law that gives employees the most rights or protections in the case of a conflict of employment laws.

Constructive discharge: "Voluntary" resignation caused by intolerable changes in working conditions caused by the employer.

Contingency fee: An attorney's fee, which is based on a percentage or fraction, usually one-third, of the amount recovered, rather than an hourly or flat rate fee.

Continuation: The right of employees, under COBRA, to remain on their employer's group health insurance policy after termination, usually for up to 18 months.

Contributory negligence: A legal theory that reduces a damage award if the plaintiff's negligence contributed to his or her own injury.

Conversion: The right of an employee, following the expiration of his or her right of continuation of group health insurance under COBRA, to convert to an individual policy.

Court costs: The fees required to bring a lawsuit, including the fee for filing the action in a specific court; often awarded to the victorious party in addition to other relief.

De minimis: Minor, as a de minimis violation of the Occupational Safety and Health Act.

Defamation: An oral or written statement impugning a person's character. *See also* Libel; Slander.

Defendant: The person or entity being sued by another person or entity (the plaintiff). *See also* Plaintiff.

Defined benefit plan: A pension plan in which a specified payout is guaranteed on retirement; the employer's contribution may vary depending on market conditions.

Defined contribution plan: A pension plan in which the employer's contribution is fixed, but the payout may vary depending on market conditions.

Deposition: A statement taken under oath prior to trial.

Disparate impact: A negative effect, as of a work rule that falls more heavily on one group than on another.

Disposable earnings: The net amount of wages remaining after lawful deductions, such as for taxes, social security, health insurance, and pension contributions.

Docking: The practice, prohibited by the Fair Labor Standards Act, of paying employees for fewer hours than they actually worked as a form of punishment (e.g., for being late for work).

Dual-purpose rule: A theory that makes an employee who is injured on a trip with both business and personal purposes eligible for workers compensation if business was the dominant purpose of the trip.

EEOC: *See* Equal Employment Opportunity Commission.

Employment at will: A noncontractual employment relationship in which the employer is free to fire the employee for any reason or no reason and the employee is free to quit with no contractual obligation.

Employment eligibility: Legal qualification to work, as in, to work in the United States.

Employment Retirement Income Security Act (ERISA): Provides federal standards or retirement plans.

Equal Employment Opportunity Commission (EEOC): A federal agency whose mandate is to administer and enforce civil rights laws.

ERISA. *See* Employment Retirement Income Security Act.

Essential function of the job: The primary duties of a job, as opposed to its incidental duties.

Et seq. (Et sequens): *And the following;* a citation reference, for example, Title 29, *U.S. Code*, sec. 100 et seq., meaning the cited material begins at Section 100 and continues for an unspecified number of sections following it.

Exempt employees: Employees who are not subject to the minimum wage and overtime provisions of the Fair Labor Standards Act, such as white-collar employees.

Experience rate: An unemployment insurance premium based on an employer's turnover rate.

Fair Labor Standards Act (FLSA): Governs federal wage and hour laws.

Federal Unemployment Tax Act (FUTA): The act under which employers are obligated to pay federal unemployment taxes.

Fellow-servant rule: An antiquated rule of law that required an employee who was injured by the actions of a coworker to sue the coworker for damages, rather than their employer.

Fetal protection policy: A company rule prohibiting women of childbearing age from working in certain hazardous jobs; ruled unconstitutional by the U.S. Supreme Court in *United Auto Workers v. Johnson Controls, Inc.*, 1991.

FLSA. *See* Fair Labor Standards Act.

Four-fifths rule: An Equal Employment Opportunity Commission guideline that says a preemployment test has an adverse impact if the selection rate for any group is less than four-fifths or 80 percent of the group with the highest selection rate; also known as the "80 percent rule."

Fringe benefits: An indirect benefit that is part of an employee's total compensation in exchange for work performed; paid parking, reduced cost or free membership in a health club, and free checking accounts are examples of fringe benefits.

Front pay: A damage award that pays a discharged employee the additional pay he or she would have earned if reinstated; usually awarded in situations where someone else has already been hired for the job.

FUTA. *See* Federal Unemployment Tax Act.

Garnishment: The attachment of wages or other money due to an individual to pay a debt.

Going and coming rule: The rule of law that says an employee who is injured during his or her normal commute to and from work is not eligible for workers compensation benefits.

Grandfather clause: A provision in a law or rule that exempts from coverage anyone who has engaged in a practice since prior to passage of the law or rule that prohibits the conduct.

Gross misconduct: A breach of work rules or behavioral standards that is so substantial as to warrant immediate discharge.

Handicap: A limitation in the capacity to perform one or more of life's major functions, such as breathing, walking, seeing, hearing, working, and so on.

Hostile working environment: An environment created by a pattern or practice of unwelcome behavior, usually sexually or racially motivated, that unreasonably interferes with an individual's job performance.

Hours worked: All hours that an employee is either required or allowed to work and for which he or she must be paid under the Fair Labor Standards Act.

Illegal alien: A foreign national not legally eligible to work in the United States.

Implied contract: A contract that is suggested by the actions of the parties involved as opposed to any specific written document or oral agreement.

Immigration and Naturalization Service (INS): The government agency that administers and enforces the Immigration Reform and Control Act.

Immigration Reform and Control Act (IRCA): The act outlines eligibility and verification requirements for legal employment in the United States.

I-9 form: The Employment Eligibility Verification Form, which must be filled out by all employees and employers in order to establish an individual's eligibility to work in the United States.

INS. *See* Immigration and Naturalization Service.

IRCA. *See* Immigration Reform and Control Act.

Just cause: A legitimate reason, as opposed to an illegal or discriminatory reason (e.g., fired for just cause).

Labor-Management Relations Act (LMRA): Also called the Taft-Hartley Act, this act governs the relationship between unions and employers.

Last-straw doctrine: The principle that, for an employee to be ineligible for unemployment compensation benefits based on discharge for repeated willful misconduct, the final act, or "last straw," must also have been willful misconduct.

Legal holidays: Paid days off traditionally given to employees for major holidays; not required to be given by private employers unless spelled out in an employment or union contract.

Libel: Defamation that is in writing.

Light duty: A nonphysical or less physical alternate work assignment offered to a workers compensation claimant to allow the employee to return to work prior to full recovery.

Liquidated damages: Damages awarded in an amount that is preset or calculated exactly rather than damages awarded that are only estimates. For example, in an age discrimination suit, damages could be established to be back pay from the time of discrimination to the present, which would be an exact amount.

LMRA. *See* Labor-Management Relations Act.

Mitigation of damages: The obligation to minimize the amount of damages insofar as possible. For example, the fired employee who is seeking damages should have made reasonable efforts to find a new job, thus reducing the amount of damages sought in a back pay award.

National Labor Relations Board (NLRB): The board charged by law with administering and enforcing the National Labor Relations Act.

National Labor Relations Act: A federal law that defines and regulates the relationship between employers and unions.

National origin: Characteristic of the nation from which one originates.

Negligent hiring: A legal concept whereby an employer knowingly or unknowingly hires an individual with a criminal background and places him or her in a situation where the opportunity is presented for the employee to commit a crime against a customer or client. For example, hiring an individual with a history of rape convictions to enter customers' homes to install cable television could result in a legal judgment of negligent hiring against the employer if that individual commits rape.

NLRB. *See* National Labor Relations Board.

Occupational Safety and Health Act (OSHA): This act regulates safety and health in the workplace.

Occupational Safety and Health Administration: This agency of the federal government administers and enforces the Occupational Safety and Health Act.

OFCCP. *See* Office of Federal Contract Compliance Programs.

Office of Federal Contract Compliance Programs (OFCCP): This office oversees federal contractors' compliance with equal employment opportunity laws. Universities with federally funded contracts fall within the jurisdiction of the OFCCP.

On-call time: The time during which an employee must be available to report to work on short notice and for which the employee must be paid if the employer requires that the employee wait in a designated place.

OSHA. *See* Occupational Safety and Health Act.

Permanency award: Payment made to an employee for permanent incapacity as a result of an on-the-job injury or illness; often based on a schedule of injuries.

Permanent injunction: A court order that requires the recipient to refrain from doing something that may cause harm if allowed to continue.

Plaintiff: The person or entity who is bringing a legal action against another person or entity, the defendant. *See Also* Defendant.

Predetermination hearing: The initial informal workers compensation hearing, which is conducted to determine the merits of a contested claim for benefits.

Preexisting condition: An injury or condition an individual had before the employee's hiring or before the current injury or condition; usually related to insurance coverage.

Preliminary injunction: A court order issued pending the final outcome of litigation that requires the recipient to refrain from doing something that may cause harm if allowed to continue.

Pretext: An excuse or rationale that covers the real reason for an employment decision.

Prima facie case: The basic evidence that "on its face" establishes grounds for a lawsuit. For example, a prima facie case of age discrimination would require evidence that the alleged victim was over the age of 40 and negative employment action was taken under circumstances that would tend to show it was for that reason.

Profit-sharing: A retirement plan in which employer contributions are tied to company profits.

Protected group/class: People who, because of historic class discrimination, are given extra protections by the law (e.g., laws that prohibit discrimination based on race, ethnicity, religion, sex, age, or disability).

Punitive damages: Damages awarded to a victim by a court as a means of penalizing the wrongdoer over and above compensatory damages.

Qualified disabled person: An individual whose disability substantially limits his or her ability to work but who is still able to perform the essential duties of the job.

Quotas: Employment practices that aim to hire in strict conformity with the statistical makeup of the local workforce (e.g., hiring persons of a particular race because that race is statistically underrepresented in the company's workforce compared to its representation in the local workforce).

Reasonable person standard: The measurement by which courts often judge a person's actions; for example, would a reasonable person have acted or been affected in the same way?

Reasonable woman standard: The measurement by which courts often judge sexual harassment claims; for example, would a reasonable woman have acted or been affected in the same way?

Recognized hazard: A dangerous condition of a particular job or industry that is generally acknowledged to exist despite reasonable safety precautions.

Reverse discrimination: Employment practices that unfairly disadvantage traditionally unprotected groups, such as whites and/or males.

Scope of employment: The range of an employee's job duties. For example, if something occurs within the scope of someone's employment, it happens while the employee is doing something reasonably connected with the employee's job.

Secondary boycott: A refusal to work for or patronize a company that continues to do business with an employer with whom a union is involved in a labor dispute. A secondary boycott is considered an unfair labor practice.

Sexual harassment: Unwelcome sexual advances, the acceptance of which is either expressly or implicitly made a condition of employment; sexually oriented behavior that creates a hostile working environment.

Slander: Verbal defamation.

Speak English-only rule: A workplace rule that requires employees to speak only English on the job. This rule is usually unlawful unless it is restricted to specific situations, such as face-to-face contact with customers who are English speakers.

Special errand: The act of reporting to work while on "on-call" status.

Special hazard: The risk associated with work as opposed to everyday risks faced by the general public.

Statute of frauds: The law providing that a contract for a term of longer than a year must be in writing to be enforceable.

Statute of limitations: The legal time limit for bringing a lawsuit or filing a lawful claim.

Stock options: A retirement plan in which employees are either given stock in the company they work for or given the option of purchasing stock in the company.

Strike: A work stoppage designed to force an employer to submit to workers' demands.

Subpoena: A legal summons requiring an individual to appear in court for a specific purpose.

Suitable work: Employment that reasonably matches an individual's qualifications, education, and experience, an offer of which, if refused, generally cuts off the person's eligibility for unemployment compensation benefits.

Taft-Hartley Act: The law that governs the relationship between unions and employers; also called the Labor-Management Relations Act.

Taxable wage base: That part of each employee's wages used to determine the employer's unemployment compensation tax liability.

Temporary partial disability: A physical impairment that causes an individual to be partially incapable of full employment for a limited period of time.

Temporary permanent disability: A physical impairment that causes an individual to be totally incapable of working for a limited period of time. Usually followed by a period of temporary partial disability.

Timeliness: The bringing of a legal action or filing of a legal claim within the time limit set by law.

Title VII: The section of the Civil Rights Act of 1964 that prohibits employers from discriminating on the basis of age, race, sex, color, religion, or national origin.

Undue hardship: An unreasonable burden, usually economic, that relieves an employer from being required to accommodate an individual's disability.

Union shop: A clause in a collective bargaining agreement that states that an employer may hire nonunion members but that they must join the union within a specified period of time, often 30 days.

Validation: A means of verifying the alleged nondiscriminatory effect of preemployment tests or other selection procedures.

Vesting: The establishment of an absolute right of ownership of the contributions made by and for the employee in a retirement plan.

Vietnam-Era Veterans' Readjustment Assistance Act: A law that requires that employers give preference in hiring and promotion to Vietnam veterans who served at least 180 days and were not dishonorably discharged and special disabled veterans who have at least a 30 percent military disability.

Vietnam-era veteran: A veteran who served in the military during the Vietnam War during the period from August 5, 1964, to May 7, 1975, and who must be given preference in work on federal government contracts and in hiring and promotion under the Vietnam Era Veterans' Readjustment Assistance Act.

Waiting time: The time an employee is required to remain at the workplace waiting to work, for example, because of a power outage, and for which the employee must be paid.

Waiver: An agreement to forgo a right conferred upon a person by law.

Weakened resistance: A theory that bases eligibility for workers compensation benefits for a nonwork injury or illness on lowered resistance caused by work.

Whistle-blower: An employee who reports an employer's violation of the law and who is protected by law from retaliation by the employer.

White-collar exemption: The exemption of executive, administrative, and professional employees from the minimum wage and overtime provisions of the Fair Labor Standards Act.

Willful misconduct: Unsuitable behavior that is engaged in either intentionally or with reckless disregard for the consequences. Discharge for repeated willful misconduct can be cause for denial of unemployment compensation benefits.

Wrongful discharge: The termination or firing of an employee in violation of the law or public policy or in breach of a written or implied employment contract.

Bibliography: Library
and Management Classics

Babbage, Charles. *On the Economy of Machinery and Manufactures.* Philadelphia: Carey & Lea, 1832.

Barnard, Chester I. *The Functions of the Executive.* Cambridge, Mass.: Harvard University Press, 1938.

Fayol, Henri. *General and Industrial Management.* London: Pitman, 1967.

Follett, Mary Parker. *Creative Experience.* New York: Longmans, Green, 1924.

Gantt, Henry L. *Organizing for Work.* New York: Harcourt, Brace and Howe, 1919.

Gilbreth, Frank B. *Primer of Scientific Management.* New York: Van Nostrand, 1912.

Herzberg, Frederick. *The Motivation to Work.* New York: Wiley, 1959.

Mayo, Elton. *The Human Problems of an Industrial Civilization.* Cambridge, Mass.: Harvard University Press, 1933.

Owen, Robert. "An Address to the Superintendents of Manufactories." In *A New View of Society.* New York: Bliss & White, 1825.

Riesman, David. *The Lonely Crowd.* New Haven, Conn.: Yale University Press, 1950.

Taylor, Frederick W. *The Principles of Scientific Management.* New York: Harper, 1911.

Wiener, Norbert. *The Human Use of Human Beings.* Boston: Houghton-Mifflin, 1950.

Wilson, Louis Round, and Maurice F. Tauber. *The University Library*, 2nd ed. New York: Columbia University Press, 1956.

■■■■■■■ Index